The No-Fail Einkorn Cookbook for Family

A Step-by-Step Guide with Healthy and Budget-Friendly Recipes, Hydration Tips and Classic Dishes Reinvented for Better Taste and Easier Digestion

Clara Elowen Hart

© Copyright 2025 by Clara Elowen Hart - All rights reserved.

The purpose of this text is to present accurate and trustworthy information on the facts and topic covered. from a policy statement that was equally accepted and authorized by an American Bar Association committee and a committee of associations and publishers.

This text may not be reproduced, duplicated, or distributed in any way, whether in print or electronic format. All rights protected.

Since all of the material presented here is accurate and consistent, the recipient and reader bear full responsibility for any liability resulting from the use or abuse of any procedures, guidelines, or directions in this document, whether due to negligence or other causes. In no event will the publication be held accountable for any recovery, damages, or monetary loss that can be directly or indirectly linked to the material presented here.

Each author is the owner of any copyrights not owned by the publisher.

Since the material presented here is intended solely for informative purposes, it can be applied broadly. The information is provided without any type of contract or guarantee.

Unauthorized use of trademarks occurs, when trademarks are published without the owner's consent or approval. The brands and trademarks in this book are all owned by their respective owners and are solely used for illustration purposes; they are not associated with this book.

Table of Content

CHAPTER 1: EINKORN DEMYSTIFIED – EVERYTHING YOU NEED TO KNOW BEFORE YOU BAKE . 7

- What is Einkorn? Understanding the World's Oldest Wheat 7
- Why Einkorn Is Better for Your Gut, Energy, and Family Health 8
- Einkorn vs. Modern Wheat: Gluten, Nutrition, and Digestibility 9
- Whole Grain vs. All-Purpose Einkorn Flour: When and How to Use Each 10
- Essential Pantry Setup: Tools, Flours, and Family-Friendly Staples 11
- Einkorn 101: Troubleshooting Sticky Dough, Wet Batters, and Dense Breads 13

CHAPTER 2: QUICK-START BREAKFASTS – NOURISHING MORNINGS MADE SIMPLE 15

- 5-Minute Einkorn Blender Pancakes 15
- One-Bowl Cinnamon Swirl Einkorn Muffins 16
- Savory Einkorn Breakfast Skillet Bread 16
- Golden Apple Einkorn Breakfast Bake 17
- No-Fail Einkorn Waffles with Greek Yogurt Crunch 17
- Maple-Glazed Einkorn Oat Bars 18
- Eggy Einkorn Toast Cups 18
- Blueberry Einkorn Sheet Pan Pancakes 19
- Einkorn Chia Waffles with Berry Compote 19
- Einkorn Breakfast Pizza with Turkey Sausage & Cheddar 20
- Creamy Einkorn Porridge with Almond Butter Drizzle 20
- Banana Bread Overnight Einkorn 21
- Veggie-Stuffed Einkorn Mini Frittata Muffins 21
- Pumpkin Spice Einkorn Breakfast Cookies 22
- Apple-Cheddar Einkorn Breakfast Biscuits 22
- Einkorn Cinnamon Swirl Breakfast Loaf 23
- Einkorn Veggie-Packed Mini Muffin Bites (Toddler-Approved) 23

CHAPTER 3: EVERYDAY ESSENTIALS – SIMPLE BREADS, ROLLS & SANDWICH STAPLES 24

- No-Knead Einkorn Sandwich Loaf 24
- 1-Hour Einkorn Dinner Rolls 25
- Soft Einkorn Burger Buns 25
- Everyday Einkorn Flatbread 26
- Cheesy Einkorn Garlic Pull-Aparts 26
- Einkorn Pita Pockets 27
- Quick Einkorn English Muffins 27
- Whole Grain Einkorn Wraps 28

Honey-Oat Einkorn Sandwich Bread 28
Einkorn Biscuit Sliders 29
Seedy Einkorn Toasting Bread 29
Einkorn Bagels Made Simple 30
Rustic Einkorn Baguettes 30
Mini Einkorn Breadsticks for Dipping 31
Einkorn Grilled Cheese Wafflewiches 31

CHAPTER 4: EINKORN SOURDOUGH WITHOUT THE STRESS – A BEGINNER'S BLUEPRINT 32

No-Fuss Einkorn Sourdough Starter from Scratch 32
Simple Everyday Einkorn Sourdough Loaf 33
Einkorn Sourdough Pizza Crust 33
Einkorn Sourdough Breakfast Muffins with Blueberry Burst 34
Einkorn Sourdough Crackers with Sea Salt 34
Slow-Rise Einkorn Sourdough Focaccia 35
Einkorn Sourdough Discard Muffins 35
Einkorn Sourdough Tortillas 36
Classic Einkorn Country Boule 36
Crispy Einkorn Sourdough Waffles 37
Einkorn Sourdough Garlic Knots 37
Einkorn Discard Flatbreads for Snacking 38
Einkorn Sourdough Cinnamon Rolls 38
Einkorn Dutch Oven Artisan Loaf 39
Einkorn Sourdough Bagels 39

CHAPTER 5: FAMILY DINNERS REINVENTED – FROM CASSEROLES TO COMFORT FOOD 40

One-Pot Einkorn Mac & Cheese Bake 40
Einkorn Crust Chicken Pot Pie 41
Savory Einkorn Veggie Galette 41
Baked Einkorn Ziti with Ricotta Swirls 42
Einkorn Crusted Meatloaf Minis 42
Weeknight Einkorn Chicken Tenders 43
Creamy Einkorn Mushroom Stroganoff 43
Einkorn Taco Pie with Corn & Black Beans 44
Sloppy Joe Einkorn Sliders 44
Einkorn-Crusted Baked Fish Sticks 45
Skillet Einkorn Tamale Bake 45
Einkorn Pasta Alfredo with Spinach & Peas 46
Einkorn Veggie Nuggets for Picky Eaters 46
Einkorn BBQ Chicken Flatbread 47

- Einkorn Stuffed Bell Peppers 47
- Rustic Einkorn Shepherd's Pie 48
- Einkorn Broccoli Cheddar Bake 48
- Crispy Einkorn Topped Casserole (Any Protein) 49
- Einkorn Sweet Potato Gnocchi 49
- Einkorn Savory Pancake Wraps with Turkey & Veggies 50

CHAPTER 6: SWEET TREATS & SPECIAL OCCASIONS – BAKING THAT FEELS LIKE A HUG 51

- Einkorn Chocolate Chunk Celebration Cake 51
- Soft-Baked Einkorn Snickerdoodle Bars 52
- Einkorn Strawberry Shortcake Biscuits 52
- Brown Butter Einkorn Blondies 53
- Einkorn Pumpkin Pie Bars 53
- Einkorn Almond Butter Brownie Bites 54
- Carrot Cake Einkorn Cupcakes with Cream Cheese Swirl 54
- Einkorn Apple Fritter Loaf 55
- Lemon Glazed Einkorn Sugar Cookies 55
- Einkorn Berry Crumble Squares 56
- Einkorn Churro Muffins 56
- Classic Einkorn Birthday Sheet Cake 57
- Einkorn Cinnamon Sugar Donut Holes (Baked) 57
- Einkorn S'mores Cookie Bars 58
- Einkorn Pear & Ginger Galette 58

CHAPTER 7: NOURISH & THRIVE – GLUTEN-SENSITIVE, ALLERGY-FRIENDLY, AND CLEAN EATING RECIPES 59

- Einkorn Oat-Free Energy Cookies 59
- Dairy-Free Einkorn Banana Muffins 60
- Einkorn Veggie Patties with Avocado Sauce 60
- Low-Sugar Einkorn Zucchini Bread 61
- Einkorn Breakfast Bars with Sunflower Seeds 61
- Einkorn "Cheesy" Pasta Bake (Dairy-Free) 62
- Einkorn Lentil Sloppy Joes 62
- Gluten-Light Einkorn Wraps with Hummus & Veggies 63
- Einkorn & Chickpea Protein Bites 63
- Einkorn Spring Roll Bowls with Ginger Dressing 64
- Einkorn Sweet Potato Breakfast Hash 64
- Einkorn Noodle Stir-Fry with Coconut Aminos 65
- Einkorn Flatbread Tacos (Allergy-Friendly Shells) 65
- Einkorn Carrot-Apple Snack Cake (No Refined Sugar) 66

- Einkorn Chia Seed Pudding Cups with Crumble Topping 66
- Einkorn Green Veggie Fritters 67
- Einkorn Black Bean Burger Sliders 67
- Einkorn Almond-Free "Granola" Clusters 68

CHAPTER 8: THE EINKORN LIFESTYLE – MEAL PLANNING, STORAGE, AND LONG-TERM SUCCESS 69

- How to Plan a Weekly Einkorn Menu for the Whole Family 69
- Einkorn Batch Cooking: What Freezes Well (and What Doesn't) 70
- Storing Einkorn Grains and Flour for Maximum Freshness 71
- Building a Family Einkorn Routine with Kids 72

Chapter 1: Einkorn Demystified – Everything You Need to Know Before You Bake

Einkorn asks you to slow down, pay attention, and unlearn the shortcuts of modern baking. It's not just flour—it's a return to food with texture, depth, and meaning. Before you measure or mix, knowing what you're working with will shape every loaf, every bite, and every choice you make.

What is Einkorn? Understanding the World's Oldest Wheat

Einkorn isn't just another "ancient grain" buzzing through health blogs—it's the oldest form of cultivated wheat known to man, dating back over 10,000 years. Before hybridization, before industrial milling, before food got complicated, there was Einkorn. Its name literally means "one grain," and it refers to the way the kernels attach to the stalk: one grain per spikelet. Primitive, sure. But that's exactly the point. Einkorn is wheat in its most unaltered, pure state.

What makes Einkorn different isn't just its age—it's its structure. Einkorn has only 14 chromosomes, compared to the 42 chromosomes found in modern wheat. That difference isn't just science trivia—it deeply affects the way Einkorn behaves in your kitchen and how it interacts with your body. Fewer chromosomes mean simpler gluten structure. That's why Einkorn doesn't stretch or rise like typical wheat, and why it's often better tolerated by people who struggle with digesting conventional flours.

If you've ever worked with modern wheat dough and expected it to behave like a stretchy balloon, Einkorn will surprise you. Its gluten is weaker and water absorption is lower, which means it won't give you the same resistance or bounce. The dough tends to be stickier, looser, more rustic. But in that texture lies its charm. It's earthy, fragrant, and deeply satisfying once you stop trying to control it and start learning how it moves.

Einkorn also has a distinctly rich, nutty flavor—somewhere between roasted almonds and fresh wheatgrass. It's not neutral like white flour. It shows up. In pancakes, it adds warmth. In bread, it brings subtle sweetness. In cookies, it enhances depth without relying on sugar. That's part of why so many families love it: you get flavor without needing much else.

But with all its benefits, Einkorn isn't a plug-and-play swap for regular flour. That's a common mistake. You can't just replace it one-for-one and expect perfect results. It absorbs less liquid. It needs shorter kneading. And it doesn't respond well to overmixing—the more you work it, the denser it becomes. You have to handle it gently, let it guide you. Think less "forceful baker," more "curious partner."

Einkorn also has a naturally higher protein content and more antioxidants, including lutein and beta-carotene. But those are just nutritional footnotes. What really matters in a family kitchen is how it feels to work with, how your kids respond to it, how it smells when it's baking. Einkorn invites you to slow down, to let go of perfection, and to rediscover the rhythm of real food.
It's not easier. But it is better—if you're willing to meet it where it is.

Why Einkorn Is Better for Your Gut, Energy, and Family Health

Einkorn's benefits aren't a trend—they're tied to its untouched, original structure. This grain hasn't been hybridized, modified, or reshaped to fit industrial-scale baking. That matters. Because the way wheat is grown and bred directly impacts how your body reacts to it.

Let's start with the gut—because that's where most people feel the difference first. Modern wheat tends to hit the digestive system like a bulldozer: fast-acting, hard to break down, often leaving people bloated, sluggish, or worse. Einkorn works differently. It has a simpler gluten structure, which makes it less likely to irritate the intestinal lining. It's not gluten-free, but it's gluten-light in a way that your system can recognize and process more easily. That's one reason why so many families dealing with sensitivity—not celiac, but the discomfort zone in between—start feeling better after switching.

Then there's the energy factor. Einkorn contains a richer profile of essential nutrients: more B vitamins, more antioxidants like lutein, and higher levels of trace minerals like zinc and iron. But what makes it stand out isn't just the amount—it's the bioavailability. Your body doesn't have to fight to access the good stuff. The grain isn't hiding it behind layers of genetic complexity. It's there, ready to nourish, without requiring a nutritional science degree to absorb.

For kids, that can mean more balanced focus, better mood, fewer crashes after meals. For adults, more sustained energy throughout the day—without the jittery spikes and slumps that often come with refined carbs or heavily processed bread products. You won't feel full and foggy. You'll feel grounded.

And then there's the emotional layer—because family health isn't just about nutrients. It's also about rhythm, tradition, and how food makes people feel. Einkorn brings a kind of calm to the kitchen. Its slower rise, its rustic feel, its quiet rebellion against convenience—those things actually contribute to health in ways you can't measure with a label. There's something grounding about baking with a grain that hasn't been tampered with. It reconnects you to the process, and that connection—messy, tactile, imperfect—is healing in its own way.

Of course, it's not a miracle grain. If someone has a diagnosed gluten disorder, Einkorn isn't a safe workaround. And if your family is used to ultra-processed flour with high elasticity and fast bake times, there will be a learning curve. Einkorn demands attention. It asks you to listen to your body and the dough. But once you tune in, it becomes a quiet, powerful ally in building meals that support long-term wellness—without sacrificing taste, comfort, or joy.

Einkorn vs. Modern Wheat: Gluten, Nutrition, and Digestibility

Einkorn and modern wheat may share a family tree, but they don't speak the same language—biologically, nutritionally, or in the way they interact with your body. To lump them together because they're both "wheat" is like saying a flip phone and a smartphone are the same because they both make calls. Technically true, but misleading.

Modern wheat has been bred over time—aggressively and intentionally—to increase yield, stretch, and shelf life. What started as an agricultural win eventually became a digestive burden. The result is a high-gluten, high-starch, low-nutrient grain designed more for machinery than people. Einkorn, on the other hand, has never been hybridized. Its genetic structure remains untouched, with only 14 chromosomes compared to modern wheat's 42. That matters. The more chromosomes a plant has, the more complex its proteins become. And complexity isn't always a good thing—especially when your digestive system is the one doing the decoding.

Gluten is at the center of this difference. Einkorn contains gluten, yes, but not the kind you're used to. Its gluten is weaker, more delicate. It lacks the aggressive gliadin fraction that modern wheat is packed with—the very component many people react to. For those dealing with gluten sensitivity (not celiac disease, but the in-between group that feels foggy, bloated, or fatigued after eating wheat), Einkorn can be a game-changer. It digests slower. It sits more gently. It nourishes without the drama.

Nutrition is another sharp divide. Einkorn's smaller grain is densely packed with nutrients—more protein per gram, significantly more lutein, and higher levels of key minerals like magnesium and zinc. And unlike fortified wheat products, Einkorn's nutrition is naturally occurring. You're not eating something that was stripped, processed, and then artificially "enriched" afterward. The body recognizes it. It knows what to do with it.

But it's not just about what's in Einkorn—it's about what's not. No synthetic enzymes, no genetic tinkering, no shortcuts to make it more profitable. That makes a difference, especially for children, where small daily choices quietly shape long-term health. The clarity of Einkorn's structure, the absence of aggressive proteins, the digestibility—it all adds up.

Still, Einkorn isn't some flawless hero. It lacks the baking elasticity of modern wheat. It won't puff and rise the way commercial flour does. That's not a defect—it's a sign of integrity. But it means your expectations need to shift. It's not about domination in the dough. It's about learning how to work with it, not against it.

Modern wheat may be everywhere, but Einkorn has something it doesn't: restraint. Simplicity. Honesty. It's not about replicating modern baking—it's about rewiring what you think bread, pasta, and pancakes should be. When you give it space to be what it is, Einkorn shows up in a way that's surprisingly human.

Whole Grain vs. All-Purpose Einkorn Flour: When and How to Use Each

Working with Einkorn flour means understanding that not all flours are created equal—not even within Einkorn itself. There are two primary types: whole grain Einkorn flour and all-purpose Einkorn flour. Both come from the same ancient seed, but what's left in—or taken out—makes all the difference in how they behave, taste, and support your baking goals.

Whole grain Einkorn flour is just that: the entire grain, stone-ground or finely milled, with bran, germ, and endosperm all intact. It's bolder—deep gold in color, rich in aroma, and undeniably present in whatever you bake. That bran layer gives it heft. It brings complexity, texture, and a toothsome quality that modern whole wheat never quite delivers without tasting heavy or bitter. In Einkorn, the flavor leans nutty, slightly sweet, and earthy, without the harshness that often scares people off whole grains.

But with that richness comes a few trade-offs. The bran in whole grain flour interrupts the gluten network even more than Einkorn already does on its own. That means baked goods can be denser, less airy, and more sensitive to overmixing or overhydration. You'll need a gentler hand and more awareness of how the dough behaves. And if you're expecting light, fluffy sandwich bread straight out of the gate? You're setting yourself up for frustration unless you understand how to adjust. That doesn't make whole grain Einkorn difficult—it just means it asks for patience and presence.

All-purpose Einkorn flour, on the other hand, has the bran and most of the germ sifted out, leaving behind the creamy, golden interior of the grain. It's smoother, lighter, and much more forgiving in recipes where structure matters—pancakes, muffins, cookies, rolls. It's the easier entry point for most home bakers, especially families looking for a healthier swap without flipping their entire baking universe upside down. You still get the flavor, the nutrition, the digestibility—but with a little more flexibility.

What you don't get with all-purpose Einkorn is a blank slate. Even though it's refined, it's not "white flour" the way you know it. It retains character. It's a bit more absorbent than you'd expect, but still less so than modern wheat. That subtle middle ground is where a lot of the magic happens.

Choosing between the two isn't about better or worse. It's about knowing what your recipe needs—and what kind of experience you want. Hearty sandwich loaf for a slow Sunday? Whole grain. Quick birthday cupcakes your kids will devour? All-purpose. Knowing when to reach for which one is the difference between guessing and actually baking with intention. And once you feel it, once you taste it, you won't need rules—you'll just know.

Essential Pantry Setup: Tools, Flours, and Family-Friendly Staples

Baking with Einkorn doesn't require a total kitchen overhaul, but it does ask for a shift in mindset—and a few thoughtful tweaks to what you keep on hand. This isn't a grain that responds well to guesswork. If your tools are dull, your measuring is sloppy, or your pantry is built around shortcuts, Einkorn will remind you—quickly—that it doesn't play by those rules. It's not fussy, but it *is* specific. And it rewards preparation.

First, the flour itself. You'll want both whole grain and all-purpose Einkorn in your pantry—ideally stored in airtight containers, away from heat and light. Einkorn spoils faster than commercial flour because it's not bleached, bromated, or packed with preservatives. If you bake often, room temp is fine. If it's more occasional, stick it in the fridge or freezer, especially in warmer climates. That's not a maybe—it's a must if you care about freshness and flavor.

Measuring accurately matters more with Einkorn than with most other grains. Invest in a good digital kitchen scale, not just for flour but for liquids, too. Einkorn's hydration window is narrow. Too much liquid and you've got a soggy, unworkable mess. Too little and it crumbles, refusing to bind. Volume measuring just doesn't cut it here—an ounce too far in either direction can throw the whole texture off. It's not about perfection, it's about consistency. And consistency starts with the scale.

You don't need fancy mixers, but a sturdy mixing bowl with high sides and a wide base makes a difference—especially when working by hand, which Einkorn often prefers. A dough scraper becomes your best friend, not for kneading in the traditional sense, but for folding, lifting, and keeping things clean as you move through the process. If you bake bread, a cast iron Dutch oven helps lock in moisture and shape without needing a bakery-grade oven setup. If you're more into muffins, cakes, and pancakes, standard pans work just fine—just be mindful of temperature and watch closely the first time you try a new recipe. Einkorn browns fast. Not because it's burning, but because of its natural sugar content. That golden crust you see? Totally normal. But let it go five minutes too long and it turns bitter, not beautiful.

Keep your pantry stocked with family-friendly additions that play well with Einkorn's flavor: real vanilla extract, raw honey, applesauce, cinnamon, shredded coconut, nut butters, and eggs. Einkorn likes moisture and richness—it thrives in recipes with fat, flavor, and structure. It does not shine in dry, low-fat, minimalistic bakes. Think nourishing, not lean. Think hearty, not hollow.

And remember: if your pantry feels too sterile, too "diet-y," Einkorn won't behave. This is a grain that likes to be fed well—and when it is, it gives back tenfold.

Einkorn 101: Troubleshooting Sticky Dough, Wet Batters, and Dense Breads

If you've baked with Einkorn and felt like the dough was misbehaving, it wasn't you—it was the flour doing exactly what it's built to do. Einkorn doesn't follow the same playbook as conventional wheat. It's slipperier. It resists structure. It clings when you think it should pull away. And it doesn't care how many flawless loaves you've made with other flours. This is its own language. And once you learn it, everything shifts.

Let's start with stickiness. Einkorn dough feels wetter than it should, even when it's not. That's because its proteins absorb water more slowly and unevenly. You might be tempted to throw in more flour. Don't. That's the first mistake. It'll lead to dry, cakey results. Instead, give the dough time. Let it sit. Let it hydrate on its own terms. Time is the secret ingredient no label mentions. The more you rush it, the worse it behaves.

With batters—especially for quick breads or muffins—the problem flips. Einkorn batters often look thinner than what you're used to, and that's okay. Don't panic if it pours like pancake batter when you expected something scoopable. Einkorn firms up quickly in the oven. Overcompensating with flour to "thicken" the batter will rob the final bake of its tenderness and make it chalky or crumbly. Trust the process. If your recipe is balanced, it will come together where it matters—on the plate.

Dense breads are the most common complaint. You followed every step. You let it rise. You shaped it with care. And then—brick. It's not a failure. It's usually overmixing or underproofing, sometimes both. Einkorn's gluten structure is fragile. It doesn't want to be kneaded into submission. Stir gently. Fold softly. And know that it won't double in size like conventional dough. Waiting for it to do so will leave you with exhausted yeast and a gummy texture. It rises modestly. That's its style. Respect it.

Another trap: expecting spring in the oven. Einkorn doesn't do dramatic oven spring. It expands slightly, but it doesn't explode with height. You have to build the shape before it bakes. A supported pan, a banneton, even a loaf mold—it needs help holding itself up. It's not weak. It's just not inflated with false elasticity.

And here's something no one tells you: sometimes it still won't come out right. That's part of the deal. The weather, the flour batch, the eggs—Einkorn responds to variables. But when you hit it just right, when the crust sets golden and the inside pulls soft and warm with that nutty aroma—it's like a handshake from the past. You're baking with history. And history is rarely predictable. But it's always worth it.

Chapter 2: Quick-Start Breakfasts – Nourishing Mornings Made Simple

5-MINUTE EINKORN BLENDER PANCAKES

P.T.: 5 minutes (preparation), 8 minutes (cooking)

Ingr.:

- 1 cup all-purpose Einkorn flour
- 1 ripe banana
- 1 large egg
- ¾ cup whole milk
- 1 tsp aluminum-free baking powder
- 1 tbsp maple syrup
- Pinch of sea salt

Serv.: 4

Method of Cooking: Griddle or nonstick skillet

Procedure:

Combine all ingredients in a high-speed blender and blend until smooth. Let the batter rest for 2 minutes. Heat a lightly oiled nonstick skillet over medium heat. Pour ¼-cup portions and cook for 2–3 minutes per side until golden. Serve warm.

N.V.: Cal. 198 | Fat 5g | Carb. 31g | Prot. 6g

ONE-BOWL CINNAMON SWIRL EINKORN MUFFINS

P.T.: 10 minutes (preparation), 18 minutes (cooking)

Ingr.:
- 1½ cups all-purpose Einkorn flour
- ½ cup coconut sugar
- 2 tsp baking powder
- 1 large egg
- ⅔ cup plain kefir
- 1 tsp vanilla extract
- 1 tsp cinnamon

Serv.: 4

Method of Cooking: Oven-baked

Procedure:

Preheat oven to 350°F. In one bowl, whisk the egg, kefir, and vanilla extract. Stir in the flour, coconut sugar, baking powder, and cinnamon until just combined. Spoon batter into greased muffin cups. Bake for 18 minutes until a toothpick comes out clean.

N.V.: Cal. 215 | Fat 8g | Carb. 31g | Prot. 4g

SAVORY EINKORN BREAKFAST SKILLET BREAD

P.T.: 12 minutes (preparation), 20 minutes (cooking)

Ingr.:
- 1¼ cups whole grain Einkorn flour
- 1 tsp baking powder
- 2 large eggs
- ¾ cup buttermilk
- ¼ cup shredded cheddar
- ½ tsp smoked paprika
- Salt to taste

Serv.: 4

Method of Cooking: Cast-iron skillet

Procedure:

Preheat oven to 375°F. In a bowl, whisk together eggs and buttermilk. Stir in flour, baking powder, smoked paprika, and salt until just mixed. Fold in cheddar. Pour into a greased 8-inch cast-iron skillet and bake for 20 minutes until set and lightly golden.

N.V.: Cal. 235 | Fat 10g | Carb. 27g | Prot. 7g

GOLDEN APPLE EINKORN BREAKFAST BAKE

P.T.: 15 minutes (preparation), 30 minutes (cooking)

Ingr.:
- 1¼ cups all-purpose Einkorn flour
- 1 tsp cinnamon
- ½ tsp baking soda
- 1 large Honeycrisp apple, diced
- 2 large eggs
- ⅓ cup unsweetened applesauce
- ¼ cup maple syrup

Serv.: 4

Method of Cooking: Oven-baked

Procedure:

Preheat oven to 350°F. Whisk eggs, applesauce, and maple syrup in a bowl. Add flour, cinnamon, and baking soda; stir until just combined. Fold in the diced apple. Pour into a greased 8x8-inch pan and bake for 30 minutes until the center is firm.

N.V.: Cal. 245 | Fat 9g | Carb. 34g | Prot. 5g

NO-FAIL EINKORN WAFFLES WITH GREEK YOGURT CRUNCH

P.T.: 10 minutes (preparation), 10 minutes (cooking)

Ingr.:
- 1 cup all-purpose Einkorn flour
- ½ tsp baking powder
- 1 tbsp raw cane sugar
- 2 large eggs
- ¾ cup full-fat Greek yogurt
- ¼ cup filtered water
- 2 tbsp melted butter

Serv.: 4

Method of Cooking: Waffle iron

Procedure:

Whisk together the flour, baking powder, and cane sugar. In another bowl, mix the eggs, Greek yogurt, water, and melted butter. Combine the mixtures until smooth. Pour batter into a preheated waffle iron and cook until golden and crisp.

N.V.: Cal. 272 | Fat 12g | Carb. 29g | Prot. 9g

MAPLE-GLAZED EINKORN OAT BARS

P.T.: 10 minutes (preparation), 22 minutes (cooking)

Ingr.:

- 1 cup all-purpose Einkorn flour
- 1 cup rolled oats
- ¼ tsp cinnamon
- ½ cup unsweetened almond butter
- ⅓ cup maple syrup
- 1 large egg
- ¼ tsp salt

Serv.: 4

Method of Cooking: Oven-baked

Procedure:

Preheat oven to 350°F. In a bowl, mix Einkorn flour, oats, cinnamon, and salt. In another bowl, whisk together almond butter, maple syrup, and egg. Combine wet and dry ingredients until just mixed. Press evenly into an 8x8-inch parchment-lined pan and bake for 22 minutes.

N.V.: Cal. 260 | Fat 11g | Carb. 34g | Prot. 6g

EGGY EINKORN TOAST CUPS

P.T.: 12 minutes (preparation), 18 minutes (cooking)

Ingr.:

- 4 slices Einkorn sandwich bread
- 4 large eggs
- ¼ cup milk
- Salt & pepper to taste
- 2 tbsp shredded mozzarella
- 1 tbsp chopped chives
- Avocado oil spray

Serv.: 4

Method of Cooking: Oven-baked

Procedure:

Preheat oven to 375°F. Press each bread slice into a greased muffin tin cup. Whisk eggs with milk, salt, and pepper, then pour evenly into each bread cup. Top with mozzarella and chives. Bake for 18 minutes until the eggs are set.

N.V.: Cal. 185 | Fat 8g | Carb. 18g | Prot. 9g

BLUEBERRY EINKORN SHEET PAN PANCAKES

P.T.: 7 minutes (preparation), 15 minutes (cooking)

Ingr.:
- 1½ cups all-purpose Einkorn flour
- 1½ tsp baking powder
- ¼ tsp salt
- 1 cup buttermilk
- 1 large egg
- 2 tbsp oil
- ½ cup blueberries

Serv.: 4

Method of Cooking: Oven-baked

Procedure:
Preheat oven to 350°F and line a rimmed sheet pan with parchment. Whisk together Einkorn flour, baking powder, and salt. In a separate bowl, mix buttermilk, egg, and oil. Combine mixtures and pour evenly into the pan. Scatter blueberries on top and bake for 15 minutes until puffed and lightly browned.

N.V.: Cal. 220 | Fat 7g | Carb. 32g | Prot. 6g

EINKORN CHIA WAFFLES WITH BERRY COMPOTE

P.T.: 10 minutes (preparation), 10 minutes (cooking)

Ingr.:
- 1 cup all-purpose Einkorn flour
- 2 tsp chia seeds
- 1 cup oat milk
- 1 egg
- 1 tbsp maple syrup
- ½ cup frozen berries
- 1 tsp butter or coconut oil

Serv.: 4

Method of Cooking: Waffle iron + stovetop

Procedure:
Whisk flour, chia, milk, egg, and maple into a smooth batter. Preheat a waffle iron and cook until crisp. Meanwhile, heat berries and butter in a small saucepan until soft and syrupy. Serve waffles topped with warm berry compote.

N.V.: Cal. 225 | Fat 7g | Carb. 33g | Prot. 6g

EINKORN BREAKFAST PIZZA WITH TURKEY SAUSAGE & CHEDDAR

P.T.: 15 minutes (preparation), 20 minutes (cooking)

Ingr.:
- 1 cup all-purpose Einkorn flour
- ½ tsp instant yeast
- ⅓ cup warm water
- ½ tsp salt
- ¼ cup cooked turkey sausage, crumbled
- ¼ cup shredded cheddar
- 1 large egg

Serv.: 4

Method of Cooking: Oven-baked

Procedure:

Combine Einkorn flour, yeast, warm water, and salt to form a sticky dough. Let rest for 20 minutes. Preheat oven to 425°F. Stretch the dough onto a parchment-lined round, then top with turkey sausage, cheddar, and a cracked egg in the center. Bake for 20 minutes until the crust is crisp and the egg is set.

N.V.: Cal. 295 | Fat 13g | Carb. 30g | Prot. 14g

CREAMY EINKORN PORRIDGE WITH ALMOND BUTTER DRIZZLE

P.T.: 5 minutes (preparation), 15 minutes (cooking)

Ingr.:
- ½ cup cracked Einkorn berries
- 2 cups water
- ½ cup unsweetened oat milk
- 1 tsp maple syrup
- ¼ tsp cinnamon
- 1 tbsp almond butter
- Pinch of salt

Serv.: 4

Method of Cooking: Stovetop simmer

Procedure:

Bring cracked Einkorn berries and water to a boil in a saucepan. Reduce heat and simmer for 12–15 minutes, stirring occasionally until thickened. Stir in oat milk, maple syrup, cinnamon, and salt; cook for 2 additional minutes. Serve in bowls drizzled with almond butter.

N.V.: Cal. 210 | Fat 7g | Carb. 29g | Prot. 6g

BANANA BREAD OVERNIGHT EINKORN

P.T.: 5 minutes (preparation), overnight chill

Ingr.:

- ¾ cup whole grain Einkorn flakes or cracked Einkorn
- 1 cup unsweetened almond milk
- ½ ripe banana, mashed
- 1 tbsp chia seeds
- 1 tbsp maple syrup
- ¼ tsp ground cinnamon
- Pinch of salt

Serv.: 4

Method of Cooking: No-cook (overnight chill)

Procedure:

In a mason jar or bowl, mix mashed banana, almond milk, maple syrup, and cinnamon. Stir in Einkorn, chia seeds, and salt until well combined. Cover and refrigerate overnight. In the morning, give it a stir and serve chilled or slightly warmed.

N.V.: Cal. 190 | Fat 5g | Carb. 30g | Prot. 5g

VEGGIE-STUFFED EINKORN MINI FRITTATA MUFFINS

P.T.: 10 minutes (preparation), 20 minutes (cooking)

Ingr.:

- 6 large eggs
- ¼ cup cooked spinach, chopped
- ¼ cup diced bell pepper
- ¼ cup grated cheddar
- 2 tbsp all-purpose Einkorn flour
- ¼ tsp salt
- Cracked black pepper to taste

Serv.: 4

Method of Cooking: Oven-baked

Procedure:

Preheat oven to 350°F and grease a muffin tin. In a bowl, whisk eggs, salt, and pepper. Fold in veggies, cheese, and Einkorn flour. Divide mixture into muffin cups. Bake for 20 minutes, or until centers are set. Cool slightly before serving.

N.V.: Cal. 160 | Fat 10g | Carb. 4g | Prot. 12g

PUMPKIN SPICE EINKORN BREAKFAST COOKIES

P.T.: 10 minutes (preparation), 16 minutes (cooking)

Ingr.:

- 1 cup all-purpose Einkorn flour
- ½ cup canned pumpkin
- 1 egg
- ¼ cup coconut sugar
- ¼ tsp pumpkin pie spice
- ¼ tsp baking soda
- Pinch of sea salt

Serv.: 4

Method of Cooking: Oven-baked

Procedure:

Preheat oven to 350°F. In a bowl, combine pumpkin, egg, and coconut sugar. Stir in flour, baking soda, spice, and salt until a soft dough forms. Scoop small mounds onto a lined baking sheet and bake for 16 minutes, until slightly golden and firm.

N.V.: Cal. 165 | Fat 4g | Carb. 26g | Prot. 4g

APPLE-CHEDDAR EINKORN BREAKFAST BISCUITS

P.T.: 12 minutes (preparation), 20 minutes (cooking)

Ingr.:

- 1½ cups all-purpose Einkorn flour
- ½ cup shredded sharp cheddar
- ½ small apple, finely diced
- 1 tsp baking powder
- ¼ tsp salt
- ⅓ cup cold butter, cubed
- ⅓ cup whole milk

Serv.: 4

Method of Cooking: Oven-baked

Procedure:

Preheat oven to 375°F. In a mixing bowl, combine flour, baking powder, and salt. Cut in butter until crumbly. Fold in cheddar and apple. Stir in milk just until dough forms. Drop spoonfuls onto a baking sheet and bake 20 minutes until golden and fragrant.

N.V.: Cal. 240 | Fat 11g | Carb. 28g | Prot. 6g

EINKORN CINNAMON SWIRL BREAKFAST LOAF

P.T.: 12 minutes (preparation), 35 minutes (baking)

Ingr.:
- 1½ cups all-purpose Einkorn flour
- 1 tsp baking powder
- ¼ tsp salt
- 1 egg
- ½ cup milk (dairy or plant-based)
- ¼ cup maple syrup
- 1 tbsp cinnamon + 1 tbsp coconut sugar (for swirl)

Serv.: 4

Method of Cooking: Oven-baked

Procedure:
Preheat oven to 350°F. In a bowl, whisk egg, milk, and maple syrup. Stir in Einkorn flour, baking powder, and salt until smooth. Pour half the batter into a greased loaf pan. Sprinkle with half the cinnamon-sugar mixture. Add remaining batter, then top with the rest of the swirl. Use a knife to create a gentle marble effect. Bake 35 minutes or until a toothpick comes out clean. Cool before slicing.

N.V.: Cal. 260 | Fat 5g | Carb. 42g | Prot. 6g

EINKORN VEGGIE-PACKED MINI MUFFIN BITES (TODDLER-APPROVED)

P.T.: 10 minutes (preparation), 18 minutes (baking)

Ingr.:
- 1 cup all-purpose Einkorn flour
- 1 egg
- ½ cup finely grated zucchini (squeezed dry)
- ¼ cup shredded carrot
- ¼ cup milk
- ¼ tsp garlic powder
- 1 tbsp olive oil

Serv.: 4

Method of Cooking: Oven-baked

Procedure:
Preheat oven to 350°F. In a bowl, whisk egg, milk, and oil. Stir in flour, garlic powder, zucchini, and carrot. Mix until just combined. Spoon into a mini muffin tin (greased or lined) and bake for 18 minutes until golden and set. Let cool slightly before serving. Great warm or at room temp.

N.V.: Cal. 190 | Fat 7g | Carb. 24g | Prot. 5g

Chapter 3: Everyday Essentials – Simple Breads, Rolls & Sandwich Staples

NO-KNEAD EINKORN SANDWICH LOAF

P.T.: 10 minutes (preparation), 40 minutes (cooking)

Ingr.:
- 3 cups all-purpose Einkorn flour
- 1 tsp fine sea salt
- ½ tsp instant yeast
- 1¼ cups warm water
- 1 tbsp olive oil
- Avocado oil spray for loaf pan
- 1 tsp raw honey

Serv.: 4

Method of Cooking: Oven-baked

Procedure:

In a large bowl, combine flour, salt, and yeast. Add warm water, honey, and olive oil. Stir until a sticky dough forms. Cover and let rise at room temp for 8–10 hours. Preheat oven to 375°F. Spray a loaf pan and scrape dough in. Smooth top with wet hands. Bake 40 minutes until golden and set. Let cool fully before slicing.

N.V.: Cal. 225 | Fat 4g | Carb. 41g | Prot. 6g

1-HOUR EINKORN DINNER ROLLS

P.T.: 15 minutes (preparation), 20 minutes (cooking)

Ingr.:

- 2½ cups all-purpose Einkorn flour
- 2¼ tsp instant yeast
- ¾ tsp salt
- 1 tbsp maple syrup
- 1 cup warm milk
- 2 tbsp unsalted butter, melted
- 1 egg

Serv.: 4

Method of Cooking: Oven-baked

Procedure:

Combine flour, yeast, and salt in a bowl. In another bowl, whisk warm milk, egg, and maple syrup. Stir wet into dry, then add melted butter. Mix into a sticky dough. Divide into 12 balls, place in a greased pan, cover and rise 25 minutes. Bake at 375°F for 20 minutes until golden.

N.V.: Cal. 210 | Fat 6g | Carb. 33g | Prot. 6g

SOFT EINKORN BURGER BUNS

P.T.: 20 minutes (preparation), 18 minutes (cooking)

Ingr.:

- 3 cups all-purpose Einkorn flour
- 1 tbsp cane sugar
- 1 tsp salt
- 2 tsp instant yeast
- 1 cup warm water
- 1 egg + 1 yolk (divided)
- 2 tbsp melted butter

Serv.: 4

Method of Cooking: Oven-baked

Procedure:

In a bowl, combine flour, sugar, salt, and yeast. Add water, egg, and melted butter. Mix and rest dough 10 minutes. Divide into 8 rounds, place on a parchment-lined sheet, cover and rise 30 minutes. Brush with egg yolk and bake at 375°F for 18 minutes.

N.V.: Cal. 240 | Fat 7g | Carb. 37g | Prot. 7g

EVERYDAY EINKORN FLATBREAD

P.T.: 10 minutes (preparation), 12 minutes (cooking)

Ingr.:
- 2 cups all-purpose Einkorn flour
- ¾ cup plain Greek yogurt
- ½ tsp sea salt
- ½ tsp baking powder
- 2 tsp olive oil
- 2 tbsp water (if needed)
- Ghee for brushing

Serv.: 4

Method of Cooking: Cast-iron skillet

Procedure:

Mix flour, salt, baking powder in a bowl. Add yogurt and olive oil. Stir to form a shaggy dough, adding water only if needed. Divide into 6 balls, roll out, and cook on hot skillet 2 minutes per side. Brush warm breads with ghee.

N.V.: Cal. 210 | Fat 6g | Carb. 29g | Prot. 7g

CHEESY EINKORN GARLIC PULL-APARTS

P.T.: 15 minutes (preparation), 22 minutes (cooking)

Ingr.:
- 2¼ cups all-purpose Einkorn flour
- 1 tsp active dry yeast
- ¾ tsp salt
- ⅔ cup warm milk
- ¼ cup shredded mozzarella
- 2 tbsp garlic butter
- 1 tbsp chopped parsley

Serv.: 4

Method of Cooking: Oven-baked

Procedure:

Combine flour, salt, and yeast. Stir in milk to form a dough. Let rise 45 minutes. Divide into small pieces and dip in garlic butter. Layer in a greased loaf pan with mozzarella and parsley. Bake at 375°F for 22 minutes until bubbling and golden.

N.V.: Cal. 235 | Fat 8g | Carb. 32g | Prot. 6g

EINKORN PITA POCKETS

P.T.: 15 minutes (preparation), 10 minutes (cooking)

Ingr.:
- 2 cups all-purpose Einkorn flour
- 1 tsp salt
- 1 tsp instant yeast
- ⅔ cup warm water
- 1 tbsp olive oil
- 1 tsp honey
- Dusting flour

Serv.: 4

Method of Cooking: Oven-baked or cast iron

Procedure:

Combine flour, salt, and yeast. Add water, honey, and olive oil. Mix into a dough and let rise 45 minutes. Divide into 6 balls, roll thin, and bake at 450°F for 5 minutes or cook in hot cast iron until puffed. Cool before slicing.

N.V.: Cal. 210 | Fat 5g | Carb. 34g | Prot. 6g

QUICK EINKORN ENGLISH MUFFINS

P.T.: 12 minutes (preparation), 14 minutes (cooking)

Ingr.:
- 2 cups all-purpose Einkorn flour
- ¾ tsp baking soda
- ¾ cup buttermilk
- ½ tsp salt
- 1 egg
- 1 tbsp olive oil
- Cornmeal for dusting

Serv.: 4

Method of Cooking: Griddle or skillet

Procedure:

Mix flour, baking soda, and salt in a bowl. Stir in buttermilk, egg, and oil until a sticky dough forms. Dust surface with cornmeal, shape into rounds, and cook on a lightly greased skillet over low heat 7 minutes per side until golden and cooked through.

N.V.: Cal. 190 | Fat 6g | Carb. 28g | Prot. 5g

WHOLE GRAIN EINKORN WRAPS

P.T.: 10 minutes (preparation), 10 minutes (cooking)

Ingr.:
- 1½ cups whole grain Einkorn flour
- ¼ tsp salt
- ⅓ cup warm water
- 1 tbsp avocado oil
- 1 tbsp flaxseed meal
- 1 tsp apple cider vinegar
- Extra flour for rolling

Serv.: 4

Method of Cooking: Skillet

Procedure:

Stir together flour, flaxseed, and salt. Add water, oil, and vinegar to form a pliable dough. Rest 10 minutes. Divide into balls and roll thin. Cook on a hot dry skillet for 1–2 minutes per side until bubbles form. Wrap while warm.

N.V.: Cal. 170 | Fat 5g | Carb. 25g | Prot. 5g

HONEY-OAT EINKORN SANDWICH BREAD

P.T.: 15 minutes (preparation), 35 minutes (cooking)

Ingr.:
- 2½ cups all-purpose Einkorn flour
- ¼ cup rolled oats
- 2 tsp instant yeast
- 1 tsp salt
- ¾ cup warm milk
- 2 tbsp honey
- 1 tbsp butter

Serv.: 4

Method of Cooking: Oven-baked

Procedure:

Combine flour, oats, yeast, and salt. Mix milk and honey, warm slightly, then add to dry mix with butter. Knead briefly and let rise 1 hour. Press into a greased loaf pan, rise 30 more minutes, and bake at 375°F for 35 minutes until golden.

N.V.: Cal. 225 | Fat 6g | Carb. 36g | Prot. 7g

EINKORN BISCUIT SLIDERS

P.T.: 10 minutes (preparation), 18 minutes (cooking)

Ingr.:
- 2 cups all-purpose Einkorn flour
- 1 tbsp baking powder
- ½ tsp salt
- ½ cup cold butter, cubed
- ⅔ cup buttermilk
- 1 egg (for brushing)
- Flaky salt for topping

Serv.: 4

Method of Cooking: Oven-baked

Procedure:

Preheat oven to 400°F. In a bowl, whisk flour, baking powder, and salt. Cut in cold butter until crumbly. Add buttermilk and stir until dough forms. Roll and cut into small rounds. Place on a baking sheet, brush with beaten egg, sprinkle with flaky salt, and bake 18 minutes.

N.V.: Cal. 230 | Fat 11g | Carb. 28g | Prot. 5g

SEEDY EINKORN TOASTING BREAD

P.T.: 15 minutes (preparation), 40 minutes (cooking)

Ingr.:
- 2½ cups whole grain Einkorn flour
- 2 tsp instant yeast
- ¾ tsp sea salt
- 1 tbsp sunflower seeds
- 1 tbsp sesame seeds
- 1 tbsp flaxseeds
- 1 cup warm water

Serv.: 4

Method of Cooking: Oven-baked

Procedure:

Combine flour, salt, and seeds in a large bowl. Stir in yeast and warm water until a sticky dough forms. Cover and let rise for 1 hour. Shape into a loaf and place in a greased pan. Let rise again for 30 minutes. Bake at 375°F for 40 minutes until golden and firm. Cool fully before slicing.

N.V.: Cal. 240 | Fat 7g | Carb. 36g | Prot. 8g

EINKORN BAGELS MADE SIMPLE

P.T.: 20 minutes (preparation), 18 minutes (cooking)

Ingr.:
- 2¼ cups all-purpose Einkorn flour
- 1 tsp salt
- 1 tsp instant yeast
- ¾ cup warm water
- 1 tbsp honey (for boiling)
- 1 egg (for egg wash)
- Optional: poppy or sesame seeds

Serv.: 4

Method of Cooking: Boil + oven-bake

Procedure:

Mix flour, yeast, salt, and warm water into a sticky dough. Knead briefly and let rise 45 minutes. Divide into 6 balls and form into bagels. Boil each in water with honey for 30 seconds per side. Place on a parchment-lined sheet, brush with egg wash, sprinkle seeds, and bake at 400°F for 18 minutes.

N.V.: Cal. 210 | Fat 2g | Carb. 40g | Prot. 7g

RUSTIC EINKORN BAGUETTES

P.T.: 15 minutes (preparation), 25 minutes (cooking)

Ingr.:
- 3 cups all-purpose Einkorn flour
- 1 tsp instant yeast
- 1 tsp salt
- 1¼ cups warm water
- 1 tbsp olive oil
- Extra flour for dusting
- Cornmeal for baking sheet

Serv.: 4

Method of Cooking: Oven-baked

Procedure:

Combine flour, salt, yeast, and water into a soft dough. Stir in olive oil. Let rise 1½ hours, then divide and shape into 2 baguettes. Place on a cornmeal-dusted sheet and let rise again 30 minutes. Dust with flour and bake at 425°F for 25 minutes, using steam or a water tray for crust.

N.V.: Cal. 225 | Fat 4g | Carb. 39g | Prot. 6g

MINI EINKORN BREADSTICKS FOR DIPPING

P.T.: 12 minutes (preparation), 15 minutes (cooking)
Ingr.:
- 1½ cups all-purpose Einkorn flour
- ½ tsp sea salt
- 1 tsp baking powder
- ½ cup water
- 2 tbsp olive oil
- ½ tsp garlic powder
- 1 tbsp grated parmesan (optional)

Serv.: 4
Method of Cooking: Oven-baked
Procedure:
Preheat oven to 375°F. Mix flour, salt, garlic powder, and baking powder. Stir in water and olive oil until dough forms. Roll into thin sticks and place on a lined baking sheet. Sprinkle parmesan if using. Bake 15 minutes until crisp and golden. Serve warm with marinara or hummus.
N.V.: Cal. 180 | Fat 6g | Carb. 28g | Prot. 4g

EINKORN GRILLED CHEESE WAFFLEWICHES

P.T.: 10 minutes (preparation), 10 minutes (cooking)
Ingr.:
- 1 cup all-purpose Einkorn flour
- 1 tsp baking powder
- 1 egg
- ⅔ cup milk
- 1 tbsp melted butter
- ½ cup shredded cheddar
- Pinch of salt

Serv.: 4
Method of Cooking: Waffle iron
Procedure:
Whisk flour, baking powder, and salt in a bowl. In another, combine milk, egg, and melted butter. Stir wet into dry to make batter. Heat waffle iron, spoon batter and sprinkle cheese before closing. Cook until golden and crisp. Cut into halves and serve warm like grilled cheese sandwiches.
N.V.: Cal. 245 | Fat 10g | Carb. 29g | Prot. 8g

Chapter 4: Einkorn Sourdough Without the Stress – A Beginner's Blueprint

NO-FUSS EINKORN SOURDOUGH STARTER FROM SCRATCH

P.T.: 5 minutes daily for 7 days

Ingr.:
- ½ cup whole grain Einkorn flour (daily)
- ¼ cup filtered water (daily)
- Glass jar or crock with breathable cover
- Wooden or silicone spoon
- Kitchen scale
- Clean towel

Serv.: 4

Method of Cooking: Fermentation

Procedure:

On Day 1, mix ½ cup flour and ¼ cup water in a clean jar. Stir until smooth. Cover with a towel and let rest at room temp. Each day for 7 days, discard half and feed with fresh flour and water. By Day 6–7, the starter should be bubbly, fragrant, and doubling in size within 4–6 hours of feeding.

N.V.: Cal. 120 | Fat 1g | Carb. 25g | Prot. 4g

SIMPLE EVERYDAY EINKORN SOURDOUGH LOAF

P.T.: 20 minutes (preparation), 45 minutes (baking), 8 hours (fermentation)

Ingr.:
- 3 cups all-purpose Einkorn flour
- 1¼ tsp sea salt
- ¾ cup active Einkorn sourdough starter
- ¾ cup warm water
- 1 tsp honey
- Extra flour for dusting
- Olive oil for bowl

Serv.: 4

Method of Cooking: Oven-baked

Procedure:

In a large bowl, mix starter, water, honey, and flour. Stir into a soft dough. Add salt and gently fold to incorporate. Cover and bulk ferment 6 hours. Perform 2–3 stretch and folds during the first 3 hours. Shape into a round, place in a floured banneton, cover, and proof another 2 hours. Preheat oven to 450°F. Bake on a hot baking stone or in a Dutch oven for 45 minutes.

N.V.: Cal. 240 | Fat 3g | Carb. 42g | Prot. 6g

EINKORN SOURDOUGH PIZZA CRUST

P.T.: 15 minutes (preparation), 14 minutes (baking), 6 hours (fermentation)

Ingr.:
- 2 cups all-purpose Einkorn flour
- ½ cup active sourdough starter
- ¾ cup warm water
- ½ tsp sea salt
- 1 tbsp olive oil
- 1 tsp raw honey
- Cornmeal for dusting

Serv.: 4

Method of Cooking: Oven-baked

Procedure:

Mix starter, water, honey, and oil. Stir in flour and salt until dough forms. Cover and let rise 6 hours. Preheat oven to 475°F with pizza stone inside. Roll or stretch dough into a round on parchment dusted with cornmeal. Top as desired. Bake for 14 minutes until crust is puffed and edges crisp.

N.V.: Cal. 260 | Fat 5g | Carb. 41g | Prot. 7g

EINKORN SOURDOUGH BREAKFAST MUFFINS WITH BLUEBERRY BURST

P.T.: 10 minutes (preparation), 22 minutes (baking)

Ingr.:

- 1 cup sourdough discard
- 1 cup all-purpose Einkorn flour
- ½ cup unsweetened almond milk
- 1 egg
- 2 tbsp maple syrup
- 1 tsp baking powder
- ½ cup fresh or frozen blueberries

Serv.: 4

Method of Cooking: Oven-baked

Procedure:

Preheat oven to 350°F. In a mixing bowl, whisk together sourdough discard, almond milk, egg, and maple syrup. Add Einkorn flour and baking powder, mixing just until combined. Gently fold in the blueberries. Divide the batter evenly into a greased or lined muffin tin. Bake for 22 minutes, or until the tops are golden and a toothpick comes out clean. Let cool slightly before serving.

N.V.: Cal. 210 | Fat 5g | Carb. 34g | Prot. 6g

EINKORN SOURDOUGH CRACKERS WITH SEA SALT

P.T.: 12 minutes (preparation), 20 minutes (baking), 4 hours (fermentation)

Ingr.:

- 1 cup sourdough discard
- ¾ cup all-purpose Einkorn flour
- 2 tbsp olive oil
- ½ tsp dried rosemary or thyme
- ½ tsp sea salt (plus more for topping)
- 1 tbsp sesame or flax seeds (optional)
- Cold water as needed

Serv.: 4

Method of Cooking: Oven-baked

Procedure:

Mix all ingredients into a smooth dough. Cover and ferment 4 hours. Roll dough thin between two sheets of parchment. Score into squares and sprinkle with flaky salt. Bake at 325°F for 18–20 minutes until golden. Let cool before breaking into pieces.

N.V.: Cal. 180 | Fat 7g | Carb. 25g | Prot. 4g

SLOW-RISE EINKORN SOURDOUGH FOCACCIA

P.T.: 15 minutes (preparation), 30 minutes (baking), 12 hours (fermentation)

Ingr.:
- 3 cups all-purpose Einkorn flour
- ¾ cup active sourdough starter
- 1 cup warm water
- 1 tsp sea salt
- 3 tbsp olive oil
- Fresh rosemary (optional)
- Flaky salt for topping

Serv.: 4

Method of Cooking: Oven-baked

Procedure:

Stir flour, water, and starter until combined. Let rest 30 minutes, then add salt and fold gently. Bulk ferment overnight (8–10 hours). Transfer to an oiled baking pan, dimple the dough with fingers, drizzle with olive oil, and sprinkle with flaky salt and herbs. Bake at 425°F for 30 minutes until golden.

N.V.: Cal. 270 | Fat 9g | Carb. 39g | Prot. 6g

EINKORN SOURDOUGH DISCARD MUFFINS

P.T.: 10 minutes (preparation), 22 minutes (baking)

Ingr.:
- 1 cup sourdough discard
- 1 cup all-purpose Einkorn flour
- ½ cup mashed ripe banana or applesauce
- 1 egg
- ¼ cup maple syrup
- 1 tsp baking powder
- ½ tsp cinnamon

Serv.: 4

Method of Cooking: Oven-baked

Procedure:

Preheat oven to 350°F. In a bowl, mix discard, egg, syrup, and banana. Stir in flour, baking powder, and cinnamon until combined. Spoon into lined muffin tins and bake 22 minutes until set and springy. Let cool before removing.

N.V.: Cal. 210 | Fat 4g | Carb. 33g | Prot. 5g

EINKORN SOURDOUGH TORTILLAS

P.T.: 10 minutes (preparation), 10 minutes (cooking), 4 hours (fermentation)

Ingr.:
- 1 cup sourdough starter (thick)
- 1½ cups all-purpose Einkorn flour
- 2 tbsp olive oil
- ½ tsp sea salt
- 2 tbsp warm water
- Dusting flour

Serv.: 4

Method of Cooking: Skillet

Procedure:

Combine all ingredients to form a soft, non-sticky dough. Cover and ferment 4 hours. Divide into 6 balls and roll thin. Cook each on a hot dry skillet 1–2 minutes per side. Stack in a towel to stay soft.

N.V.: Cal. 185 | Fat 6g | Carb. 27g | Prot. 5g

CLASSIC EINKORN COUNTRY BOULE

P.T.: 25 minutes (preparation), 45 minutes (baking), 10 hours (fermentation)

Ingr.:
- 3½ cups all-purpose Einkorn flour
- 1¼ tsp salt
- ¾ cup active sourdough starter
- 1¼ cups filtered water
- 1 tbsp olive oil
- Rice flour for dusting
- Dutch oven

Serv.: 4

Method of Cooking: Dutch oven

Procedure:

Mix flour, water, and starter into a sticky dough. Add salt and oil, then fold gently. Bulk ferment 6–8 hours with 3 folds. Shape, place into a rice-floured banneton, and refrigerate 2–4 hours. Preheat Dutch oven to 475°F. Score dough and bake covered 25 minutes, uncovered 20 minutes.

N.V.: Cal. 250 | Fat 4g | Carb. 42g | Prot. 6g

CRISPY EINKORN SOURDOUGH WAFFLES

P.T.: 10 minutes (preparation), 10 minutes (cooking), overnight ferment

Ingr.:
- 1 cup sourdough starter
- 1 cup all-purpose Einkorn flour
- ¾ cup milk
- 1 egg
- 2 tbsp melted butter
- 1 tsp vanilla
- ½ tsp baking soda

Serv.: 4

Method of Cooking: Waffle iron

Procedure:
The night before, mix starter, flour, and milk. Cover and rest overnight. In the morning, whisk in egg, melted butter, vanilla, and baking soda. Cook in a hot waffle iron until golden and crisp. Serve immediately.

N.V.: Cal. 230 | Fat 9g | Carb. 30g | Prot. 6g

EINKORN SOURDOUGH GARLIC KNOTS

P.T.: 15 minutes (preparation), 18 minutes (baking), 6 hours (fermentation)

Ingr.:
- 2¼ cups all-purpose Einkorn flour
- ½ cup active sourdough starter
- ¾ cup warm water
- ¾ tsp sea salt
- 1 tbsp olive oil
- 2 tbsp garlic butter (for brushing)
- Chopped parsley (optional)

Serv.: 4

Method of Cooking: Oven-baked

Procedure:
Mix starter, water, and flour into a soft dough. Rest 30 minutes, add salt and oil, then stretch and fold gently. Bulk ferment 4–6 hours. Divide dough into 8 strips, tie into knots, and place on a parchment-lined sheet. Let rest 30 minutes. Bake at 400°F for 18 minutes. Brush warm knots with garlic butter and sprinkle with parsley.

N.V.: Cal. 210 | Fat 6g | Carb. 34g | Prot. 6g

EINKORN DISCARD FLATBREADS FOR SNACKING

P.T.: 10 minutes (preparation), 10 minutes (cooking)

Ingr.:
- 1 cup sourdough discard
- 1 cup all-purpose Einkorn flour
- ¼ tsp salt
- 2 tbsp olive oil
- ¼ cup warm water
- ½ tsp dried oregano or za'atar
- Extra oil for brushing

Serv.: 4

Method of Cooking: Skillet

Procedure:

Mix all ingredients into a smooth dough. Rest 10 minutes. Divide and roll thin. Heat a dry skillet over medium-high and cook each flatbread for 1–2 minutes per side until golden spots appear. Brush lightly with oil and sprinkle with herbs or finishing salt.

N.V.: Cal. 200 | Fat 7g | Carb. 29g | Prot. 5g

EINKORN SOURDOUGH CINNAMON ROLLS

P.T.: 20 minutes (preparation), 25 minutes (baking), 8 hours (fermentation)

Ingr.:
- 2½ cups all-purpose Einkorn flour
- ½ cup active sourdough starter
- ½ cup whole milk
- 1 egg
- ¼ cup maple syrup
- 1 tbsp cinnamon
- 2 tbsp soft butter (for filling)

Serv.: 4

Method of Cooking: Oven-baked

Procedure:

Mix flour, starter, milk, egg, and maple syrup into a soft dough. Bulk ferment 6 hours. Roll into a rectangle, spread with butter, and sprinkle with cinnamon. Roll up and slice into 6 pieces. Place in a greased pan, cover, and proof 2 more hours. Bake at 375°F for 25 minutes.

N.V.: Cal. 260 | Fat 8g | Carb. 38g | Prot. 6g

EINKORN DUTCH OVEN ARTISAN LOAF

P.T.: 25 minutes (preparation), 45 minutes (baking), 10 hours (fermentation)

Ingr.:
- 3½ cups all-purpose Einkorn flour
- 1 cup active sourdough starter
- 1¼ cups filtered water
- 1½ tsp salt
- Rice flour for dusting
- Olive oil for greasing
- Dutch oven with lid

Serv.: 4

Method of Cooking: Dutch oven

Procedure:

Mix flour, water, and starter until shaggy. Rest 30 minutes, then add salt and fold gently. Bulk ferment 6–8 hours, then shape into a boule. Place into a rice-floured banneton and proof 2 more hours. Preheat Dutch oven to 475°F. Score the loaf and bake covered for 25 minutes, then uncovered for 20 minutes until deeply golden.

N.V.: Cal. 250 | Fat 3g | Carb. 44g | Prot. 7g

EINKORN SOURDOUGH BAGELS

P.T.: 20 minutes (preparation), 18 minutes (baking), 6 hours (fermentation)

Ingr.:
- 2½ cups all-purpose Einkorn flour
- ½ cup active sourdough starter
- ¾ cup warm water
- 1 tsp salt
- 1 tbsp honey (for boiling)
- 1 egg (for egg wash)
- Sesame or poppy seeds (optional)

Serv.: 4

Method of Cooking: Boil + oven-bake

Procedure:

Mix starter, water, flour, and salt into a dough. Knead briefly and let rise 6 hours. Divide and shape into bagels. Boil each for 30 seconds per side in water with honey. Place on a baking sheet, brush with egg wash, and top with seeds. Bake at 425°F for 18 minutes.

N.V.: Cal. 230 | Fat 2g | Carb. 42g | Prot. 8g

Chapter 5: Family Dinners Reinvented – From Casseroles to Comfort Food

ONE-POT EINKORN MAC & CHEESE BAKE

P.T.: 10 minutes (preparation), 25 minutes (cooking)

Ingr.:

- 1½ cups Einkorn elbow pasta
- 2 cups whole milk
- 1 tbsp butter
- 1 tsp garlic powder
- 1½ cups shredded sharp cheddar
- 2 tbsp grated Parmesan
- ½ tsp Dijon mustard

Serv.: 4

Method of Cooking: Stovetop to oven

Procedure:

In a deep oven-safe skillet, combine pasta, milk, butter, garlic powder, and mustard. Bring to a simmer, stirring frequently. Cook 10–12 minutes until pasta is tender and sauce thickens. Stir in cheddar. Sprinkle Parmesan over top and broil 3 minutes until golden and bubbling.

N.V.: Cal. 430 | Fat 17g | Carb. 48g | Prot. 19g

EINKORN CRUST CHICKEN POT PIE

P.T.: 20 minutes (preparation), 35 minutes (cooking)

Ingr.:

- 1½ cups all-purpose Einkorn flour
- ½ cup cold butter, cubed
- ¼ cup ice water
- 1½ cups cooked diced chicken
- 1 cup frozen mixed vegetables
- ¾ cup chicken broth
- ¼ cup plain Greek yogurt

Serv.: 4

Method of Cooking: Oven-baked

Procedure:

Prepare crust by cutting butter into flour until crumbly. Add water until dough forms. Chill while prepping filling. In a saucepan, combine chicken, veggies, broth, and yogurt. Simmer 5 minutes. Transfer to a baking dish. Roll out crust, lay over filling, seal edges, and vent. Bake at 375°F for 35 minutes.

N.V.: Cal. 490 | Fat 25g | Carb. 38g | Prot. 26g

SAVORY EINKORN VEGGIE GALETTE

P.T.: 25 minutes (preparation), 30 minutes (cooking)

Ingr.:

- 1¼ cups all-purpose Einkorn flour
- ½ cup cold butter, cubed
- ¼ cup ice water
- 1 zucchini, thinly sliced
- 1 small red onion, sliced
- ½ cup ricotta
- 1 tsp thyme

Serv.: 4

Method of Cooking: Oven-baked

Procedure:

Make dough by blending butter into flour, then adding water until it holds together. Chill 15 minutes. Roll out into a 10-inch circle. Spread ricotta in center, layer veggies, sprinkle thyme. Fold edges inward. Bake on a lined sheet at 400°F for 30 minutes until crust is golden.

N.V.: Cal. 360 | Fat 22g | Carb. 30g | Prot. 8g

BAKED EINKORN ZITI WITH RICOTTA SWIRLS

P.T.: 15 minutes (preparation), 30 minutes (baking)

Ingr.:

- 2 cups cooked Einkorn penne
- 1½ cups marinara sauce
- ¾ cup ricotta cheese
- 1 egg
- 1 cup shredded mozzarella
- 1 tsp Italian herbs
- Olive oil spray

Serv.: 4

Method of Cooking: Oven-baked

Procedure:

Mix ricotta, egg, and herbs. Toss cooked pasta with sauce. In a greased baking dish, layer half the pasta, dot ricotta mix, top with remaining pasta, and cover with mozzarella. Bake at 375°F for 30 minutes until bubbly and golden. Let rest 10 minutes before serving.

N.V.: Cal. 410 | Fat 17g | Carb. 45g | Prot. 20g

EINKORN CRUSTED MEATLOAF MINIS

P.T.: 15 minutes (preparation), 25 minutes (baking)

Ingr.:

- 1 lb ground turkey
- ½ cup finely grated carrot
- ⅓ cup Einkorn breadcrumbs
- 1 egg
- 1 tbsp tomato paste
- 1 tsp onion powder
- 1 tsp sea salt

Serv.: 4

Method of Cooking: Oven-baked

Procedure:

Preheat oven to 375°F. In a bowl, combine all ingredients. Form into 8 mini loaves and place on a parchment-lined baking sheet. Bake 25 minutes until internal temp reaches 165°F. Serve with ketchup, gravy, or plain.

N.V.: Cal. 290 | Fat 12g | Carb. 14g | Prot. 30g

WEEKNIGHT EINKORN CHICKEN TENDERS

P.T.: 10 minutes (preparation), 20 minutes (baking)

Ingr.:
- 1 lb chicken breast tenders
- ¾ cup all-purpose Einkorn flour
- 1 egg
- 1 tsp paprika
- ½ tsp garlic salt
- ½ cup breadcrumbs
- Olive oil spray

Serv.: 4

Method of Cooking: Oven-baked

Procedure:

Preheat oven to 400°F. Set up breading station with flour, beaten egg, and breadcrumbs mixed with paprika and garlic salt. Dredge each tender in flour, egg, then breadcrumb mix. Place on greased baking sheet and spray tops with olive oil. Bake 20 minutes, flipping halfway.

N.V.: Cal. 330 | Fat 10g | Carb. 22g | Prot. 35g

CREAMY EINKORN MUSHROOM STROGANOFF

P.T.: 10 minutes (preparation), 20 minutes (cooking)

Ingr.:
- 1½ cups cooked Einkorn fusilli
- 2 cups cremini mushrooms, sliced
- 1 tbsp butter
- 1 clove garlic, minced
- ⅔ cup sour cream
- 1 tsp smoked paprika
- 1 tbsp fresh parsley

Serv.: 4

Method of Cooking: Stovetop

Procedure:

Sauté mushrooms in butter over medium heat for 6–8 minutes. Add garlic and paprika, cook 1 minute. Stir in sour cream and cooked pasta. Simmer 3 minutes until creamy. Garnish with parsley and serve warm.

N.V.: Cal. 370 | Fat 17g | Carb. 38g | Prot. 12g

EINKORN TACO PIE WITH CORN & BLACK BEANS

P.T.: 15 minutes (preparation), 25 minutes (baking)

Ingr.:
- 1 pre-baked Einkorn pie crust
- ¾ lb ground beef or turkey
- ½ cup canned black beans, rinsed
- ½ cup frozen corn
- ¾ cup salsa
- ½ tsp cumin
- ½ cup shredded Monterey Jack

Serv.: 4

Method of Cooking: Oven-baked

Procedure:

Brown meat with cumin in a skillet. Stir in salsa, beans, and corn. Simmer 5 minutes. Spoon into crust, top with cheese, and bake at 375°F for 25 minutes. Let cool slightly before slicing.

N.V.: Cal. 430 | Fat 20g | Carb. 30g | Prot. 28g

SLOPPY JOE EINKORN SLIDERS

P.T.: 12 minutes (preparation), 15 minutes (cooking)

Ingr.:
- ¾ lb ground beef
- ½ cup tomato sauce
- 1 tbsp Dijon mustard
- 1 tbsp coconut sugar
- ¼ tsp chili powder
- 1 tsp Worcestershire sauce
- 8 mini Einkorn buns

Serv.: 4

Method of Cooking: Stovetop

Procedure:

Brown beef in a skillet. Stir in tomato sauce, mustard, sugar, Worcestershire, and chili powder. Simmer 10 minutes until thickened. Spoon onto warm mini buns and serve immediately.

N.V.: Cal. 360 | Fat 13g | Carb. 35g | Prot. 22g

EINKORN-CRUSTED BAKED FISH STICKS

P.T.: 10 minutes (preparation), 18 minutes (baking)

Ingr.:

- 1 lb cod or pollock, cut into strips
- ½ cup all-purpose Einkorn flour
- 1 egg
- ½ cup Einkorn breadcrumbs
- 1 tsp lemon zest
- ½ tsp smoked paprika
- Olive oil spray

Serv.: 4

Method of Cooking: Oven-baked

Procedure:

Preheat oven to 400°F. Set up breading station with flour, beaten egg, and breadcrumbs mixed with lemon zest and paprika. Dredge fish in flour, egg, then breadcrumbs. Arrange on lined baking sheet. Spray lightly with oil and bake for 18 minutes until golden.

N.V.: Cal. 275 | Fat 7g | Carb. 20g | Prot. 30g

SKILLET EINKORN TAMALE BAKE

P.T.: 15 minutes (preparation), 25 minutes (cooking)

Ingr.:

- ¾ cup Einkorn cornmeal or finely ground Einkorn flour
- 1¼ cups milk
- 1 egg
- 1 tsp baking powder
- 1 cup cooked shredded chicken
- ½ cup enchilada sauce
- ½ cup shredded pepper jack

Serv.: 4

Method of Cooking: Stovetop to oven

Procedure:

Preheat oven to 375°F. In a skillet, whisk cornmeal, milk, egg, and baking powder. Cook over medium heat 3–4 minutes until thick. Remove from heat and spread chicken and enchilada sauce over top. Sprinkle with cheese. Bake 20–25 minutes until bubbly.

N.V.: Cal. 390 | Fat 16g | Carb. 34g | Prot. 25g

EINKORN PASTA ALFREDO WITH SPINACH & PEAS

P.T.: 10 minutes (preparation), 15 minutes (cooking)

Ingr.:
- 2 cups cooked Einkorn fusilli
- 1 tbsp butter
- ¾ cup heavy cream or cashew cream
- ½ cup baby spinach
- ⅓ cup peas (fresh or frozen)
- ½ cup grated Parmesan
- ¼ tsp garlic powder

Serv.: 4

Method of Cooking: Stovetop

Procedure:

Melt butter in a skillet, stir in cream and garlic powder. Add spinach and peas, cook until wilted. Stir in cheese and cooked pasta. Simmer 2–3 minutes until thick and creamy. Serve warm.

N.V.: Cal. 410 | Fat 21g | Carb. 36g | Prot. 15g

EINKORN VEGGIE NUGGETS FOR PICKY EATERS

P.T.: 15 minutes (preparation), 20 minutes (baking)

Ingr.:
- 1 cup mashed sweet potato
- ½ cup grated zucchini
- ½ cup shredded cheddar
- ⅓ cup all-purpose Einkorn flour
- ½ tsp onion powder
- ½ tsp sea salt
- Olive oil spray

Serv.: 4

Method of Cooking: Oven-baked

Procedure:

Preheat oven to 375°F. In a bowl, mix all ingredients until a sticky batter forms. Scoop small nugget shapes onto a lined sheet. Flatten slightly. Spray with oil and bake 20 minutes, flipping halfway. Let cool slightly before serving.

N.V.: Cal. 210 | Fat 9g | Carb. 24g | Prot. 7g

EINKORN BBQ CHICKEN FLATBREAD

P.T.: 20 minutes (preparation), 12 minutes (baking)
Ingr.:
- 1 cup all-purpose Einkorn flour
- ¼ tsp salt
- ⅓ cup Greek yogurt
- 1 tsp olive oil
- 1 cup shredded cooked chicken
- ¼ cup BBQ sauce
- ½ cup shredded mozzarella

Serv.: 4
Method of Cooking: Oven-baked
Procedure:
Preheat oven to 400°F. Mix flour, salt, yogurt, and oil into a soft dough. Roll into a thin oval. Place on a lined sheet. Spread with BBQ sauce, top with chicken and cheese. Bake 12 minutes until crust is golden and cheese bubbles.
N.V.: Cal. 360 | Fat 12g | Carb. 34g | Prot. 25g

EINKORN STUFFED BELL PEPPERS

P.T.: 20 minutes (preparation), 30 minutes (baking)
Ingr.:
- 4 bell peppers, halved and seeded
- 1½ cups cooked Einkorn grain
- 1 cup cooked lentils or ground turkey
- ½ cup tomato sauce
- 1 tsp Italian herbs
- ¼ cup grated Parmesan
- Olive oil spray

Serv.: 4
Method of Cooking: Oven-baked
Procedure:
Preheat oven to 375°F. In a bowl, combine Einkorn, protein, tomato sauce, and herbs. Fill pepper halves and place in a greased baking dish. Sprinkle Parmesan over top. Cover loosely with foil and bake 30 minutes.
N.V.: Cal. 290 | Fat 9g | Carb. 36g | Prot. 14g

RUSTIC EINKORN SHEPHERD'S PIE

P.T.: 25 minutes (preparation), 25 minutes (baking)

Ingr.:
- ¾ lb ground beef or lentils
- 1 cup chopped carrots and peas
- 2 tbsp tomato paste
- 2 cups mashed potatoes
- 1 tbsp butter
- ½ cup beef or veggie broth
- Salt and pepper to taste

Serv.: 4

Method of Cooking: Stovetop + oven-baked

Procedure:

Brown beef in a skillet, then add vegetables, paste, and broth. Simmer until thick. Spread mixture in a baking dish. Top with mashed potatoes, dot with butter. Bake at 400°F for 25 minutes until golden and bubbling.

N.V.: Cal. 370 | Fat 16g | Carb. 32g | Prot. 22g

EINKORN BROCCOLI CHEDDAR BAKE

P.T.: 15 minutes (preparation), 25 minutes (baking)

Ingr.:
- 2 cups chopped broccoli (steamed)
- 1 cup cooked Einkorn pasta
- 1 cup shredded cheddar
- ½ cup milk
- 1 tbsp Einkorn flour
- 1 tbsp butter
- ¼ tsp mustard powder

Serv.: 4

Method of Cooking: Stovetop + oven

Procedure:

In a saucepan, melt butter, whisk in flour, then milk. Stir in cheese and mustard powder. Once melted, combine with pasta and broccoli. Pour into a greased dish and bake at 375°F for 25 minutes.

N.V.: Cal. 350 | Fat 18g | Carb. 28g | Prot. 17g

CRISPY EINKORN TOPPED CASSEROLE (ANY PROTEIN)

P.T.: 15 minutes (preparation), 30 minutes (baking)

Ingr.:
- 2 cups shredded chicken, turkey, or lentils
- 1 cup steamed green beans
- 1 can cream of mushroom soup or homemade
- ½ tsp garlic powder
- ½ cup shredded cheese
- ¾ cup Einkorn breadcrumb topping
- Olive oil or butter

Serv.: 4

Method of Cooking: Oven-baked

Procedure:

Mix protein, beans, soup, and spices. Pour into a greased dish. Top with cheese. Toss breadcrumbs in oil and sprinkle over. Bake uncovered at 375°F for 30 minutes until hot and crispy.

N.V.: Cal. 400 | Fat 18g | Carb. 30g | Prot. 28g

EINKORN SWEET POTATO GNOCCHI

P.T.: 30 minutes (preparation), 10 minutes (cooking)

Ingr.:
- 1 cup mashed roasted sweet potato
- ¾ cup all-purpose Einkorn flour
- 1 egg
- ½ tsp sea salt
- Butter or sage oil for serving
- Parmesan (optional)
- Black pepper

Serv.: 4

Method of Cooking: Boiled + sautéed

Procedure:

Mix sweet potato, flour, egg, and salt into a soft dough. Roll into ropes, cut into bite-size pieces. Boil in salted water until they float. Drain, then pan-fry in butter or sage oil until lightly golden. Serve with pepper and cheese.

N.V.: Cal. 280 | Fat 8g | Carb. 41g | Prot. 8g

EINKORN SAVORY PANCAKE WRAPS WITH TURKEY & VEGGIES

P.T.: 10 minutes (preparation), 10 minutes (cooking)

Ingr.:
- ¾ cup Einkorn flour
- 1 egg
- ½ cup milk
- 1 cup cooked turkey slices
- ½ cup sautéed peppers and onions
- ½ tsp garlic powder
- Olive oil for skillet

Serv.: 4

Method of Cooking: Skillet

Procedure:

Whisk flour, egg, milk, and garlic powder until smooth. Cook thin pancakes on a greased skillet, 2 minutes per side. Fill with warm turkey and veggies. Fold and serve like wraps.

N.V.: Cal. 290 | Fat 9g | Carb. 28g | Prot. 18g

Chapter 6: Sweet Treats & Special Occasions – Baking That Feels Like a Hug

EINKORN CHOCOLATE CHUNK CELEBRATION CAKE

P.T.: 20 minutes (preparation), 30 minutes (baking)

Ingr.:
- 1½ cups all-purpose Einkorn flour
- ½ cup coconut sugar
- 1 tsp baking powder
- 2 eggs
- ½ cup Greek yogurt
- ½ cup dark chocolate chunks
- ¼ cup avocado oil

Serv.: 4

Method of Cooking: Oven-baked

Procedure:

Preheat oven to 350°F. In a bowl, whisk eggs, yogurt, and oil. Stir in flour, sugar, and baking powder until combined. Fold in chocolate chunks. Pour batter into a greased 8-inch round pan. Bake 30 minutes or until a toothpick comes out clean. Cool before slicing.

N.V.: Cal. 360 | Fat 18g | Carb. 38g | Prot. 7g

SOFT-BAKED EINKORN SNICKERDOODLE BARS

P.T.: 12 minutes (preparation), 22 minutes (baking)

Ingr.:
- 1 cup all-purpose Einkorn flour
- ½ cup coconut sugar
- ¼ cup butter, melted
- 1 egg
- ½ tsp cream of tartar
- ¼ tsp baking soda
- 1 tsp cinnamon

Serv.: 4

Method of Cooking: Oven-baked

Procedure:

Preheat oven to 350°F. Mix melted butter, sugar, and egg until smooth. Stir in flour, cream of tartar, baking soda, and half the cinnamon. Spread into an 8x8 pan. Sprinkle with remaining cinnamon. Bake for 22 minutes or until golden and set. Cool completely before slicing.

N.V.: Cal. 310 | Fat 12g | Carb. 42g | Prot. 4g

EINKORN STRAWBERRY SHORTCAKE BISCUITS

P.T.: 15 minutes (preparation), 20 minutes (baking)

Ingr.:
- 1½ cups all-purpose Einkorn flour
- 2 tbsp cane sugar
- ½ tbsp baking powder
- ½ cup cold butter, cubed
- ½ cup milk
- 1 cup sliced strawberries
- Whipped cream for serving

Serv.: 4

Method of Cooking: Oven-baked

Procedure:

Preheat oven to 375°F. In a bowl, combine flour, sugar, and baking powder. Cut in cold butter until crumbly. Stir in milk until dough forms. Drop spoonfuls onto a baking sheet. Bake 20 minutes. Split biscuits and fill with strawberries and whipped cream.

N.V.: Cal. 330 | Fat 16g | Carb. 40g | Prot. 5g

BROWN BUTTER EINKORN BLONDIES

P.T.: 15 minutes (preparation), 25 minutes (baking)

Ingr.:
- ¾ cup butter
- 1 cup coconut sugar
- 2 eggs
- 1 cup all-purpose Einkorn flour
- ½ tsp vanilla
- ¼ tsp salt
- ½ cup chopped walnuts or chocolate chips

Serv.: 4

Method of Cooking: Oven-baked

Procedure:

Melt butter in a skillet over medium heat until golden and fragrant. Let cool slightly. Mix with sugar and eggs. Stir in flour, vanilla, and salt. Fold in walnuts or chips. Pour into greased 8x8 pan. Bake at 350°F for 25 minutes.

N.V.: Cal. 400 | Fat 22g | Carb. 42g | Prot. 6g

EINKORN PUMPKIN PIE BARS

P.T.: 20 minutes (preparation), 35 minutes (baking)

Ingr.:
- 1 cup all-purpose Einkorn flour
- ¼ cup cold butter
- 2 tbsp maple syrup
- ¾ cup pumpkin puree
- 1 egg
- ¼ cup coconut milk
- 1 tsp pumpkin pie spice

Serv.: 4

Method of Cooking: Oven-baked

Procedure:

Preheat oven to 350°F. Combine flour and butter to form a crumbly crust. Press into a lined loaf pan and bake 10 minutes. Blend pumpkin, egg, maple syrup, milk, and spice. Pour over crust and bake 25 minutes until set. Cool before slicing.

N.V.: Cal. 290 | Fat 14g | Carb. 34g | Prot. 4g

EINKORN ALMOND BUTTER BROWNIE BITES

P.T.: 10 minutes (preparation), 16 minutes (baking)

Ingr.:
- ½ cup almond butter
- 2 eggs
- ½ cup coconut sugar
- ½ cup all-purpose Einkorn flour
- ¼ cup cocoa powder
- ½ tsp baking soda
- Pinch of salt

Serv.: 4

Method of Cooking: Oven-baked

Procedure:

Preheat oven to 350°F. Stir almond butter, eggs, and sugar until smooth. Add flour, cocoa, baking soda, and salt. Mix well. Spoon into greased mini muffin tins. Bake 16 minutes. Let cool slightly before removing.

N.V.: Cal. 275 | Fat 14g | Carb. 28g | Prot. 6g

CARROT CAKE EINKORN CUPCAKES WITH CREAM CHEESE SWIRL

P.T.: 15 minutes (preparation), 22 minutes (baking)

Ingr.:
- 1 cup all-purpose Einkorn flour
- ½ cup grated carrot
- ¼ cup maple syrup
- ¼ cup oil
- 1 egg
- ¼ tsp cinnamon
- ¼ cup cream cheese (softened, optional swirl)

Serv.: 4

Method of Cooking: Oven-baked

Procedure:

Preheat oven to 350°F. Mix oil, egg, and syrup. Stir in flour, carrot, and cinnamon. Spoon into lined cupcake tins. Drop a teaspoon of cream cheese on top of each and swirl lightly. Bake 22 minutes until set and golden.

N.V.: Cal. 295 | Fat 13g | Carb. 36g | Prot. 5g

EINKORN APPLE FRITTER LOAF

P.T.: 15 minutes (preparation), 35 minutes (baking)
Ingr.:
- 1½ cups all-purpose Einkorn flour
- ½ tsp baking soda
- ½ tsp cinnamon
- ½ cup maple syrup
- 1 egg
- ¼ cup milk
- 1 apple, peeled and chopped

Serv.: 4
Method of Cooking: Oven-baked
Procedure:
Preheat oven to 350°F. Mix flour, soda, and cinnamon in a bowl. In another bowl, combine egg, syrup, and milk. Add wet to dry and fold in apples. Pour into a greased loaf pan and bake 35 minutes until center is firm. Cool 15 minutes before slicing.
N.V.: Cal. 310 | Fat 6g | Carb. 50g | Prot. 5g

LEMON GLAZED EINKORN SUGAR COOKIES

P.T.: 15 minutes (preparation), 12 minutes (baking)
Ingr.:
- 1 cup all-purpose Einkorn flour
- ¼ cup butter, softened
- ⅓ cup cane sugar
- 1 egg yolk
- 1 tsp lemon zest
- ½ tsp vanilla
- ¼ cup powdered sugar + lemon juice (for glaze)

Serv.: 4
Method of Cooking: Oven-baked
Procedure:
Preheat oven to 350°F. Cream butter, sugar, and egg yolk. Add zest and vanilla, then mix in flour until dough forms. Roll into balls and flatten slightly on a baking sheet. Bake 12 minutes. Cool and drizzle with lemon glaze.
N.V.: Cal. 240 | Fat 10g | Carb. 34g | Prot. 3g

EINKORN BERRY CRUMBLE SQUARES

P.T.: 15 minutes (preparation), 30 minutes (baking)
Ingr.:
- 1¼ cups all-purpose Einkorn flour
- ½ cup rolled oats
- ¼ cup coconut oil or butter
- ¼ cup maple syrup
- 1½ cups mixed berries (fresh or frozen)
- 1 tbsp tapioca flour
- 1 tsp lemon juice

Serv.: 4
Method of Cooking: Oven-baked
Procedure:
Preheat oven to 350°F. In a bowl, mix flour, oats, and oil. Add syrup and mix into crumbles. Press ⅔ into a lined pan. Toss berries with lemon juice and tapioca flour, then spread over crust. Sprinkle remaining crumble on top. Bake 30 minutes.
N.V.: Cal. 280 | Fat 11g | Carb. 39g | Prot. 4g

EINKORN CHURRO MUFFINS

P.T.: 15 minutes (preparation), 20 minutes (baking)
Ingr.:
- 1½ cups all-purpose Einkorn flour
- ½ cup cane sugar
- 1 tsp baking powder
- ½ tsp cinnamon
- 1 egg
- ½ cup milk
- ¼ cup butter, melted

Serv.: 4
Method of Cooking: Oven-baked
Procedure:
Preheat oven to 350°F. In a bowl, whisk together sugar, egg, milk, and butter. Stir in flour, baking powder, and cinnamon until just combined. Spoon into greased or lined muffin tins and bake for 20 minutes. While still warm, brush tops with butter and roll in cinnamon sugar if desired.
N.V.: Cal. 280 | Fat 12g | Carb. 38g | Prot. 4g

CLASSIC EINKORN BIRTHDAY SHEET CAKE

P.T.: 20 minutes (preparation), 30 minutes (baking)

Ingr.:
- 2 cups all-purpose Einkorn flour
- ¾ cup cane sugar
- 1 tsp baking soda
- 2 eggs
- ¾ cup yogurt or sour cream
- ½ cup neutral oil
- 1 tsp vanilla extract

Serv.: 4

Method of Cooking: Oven-baked

Procedure:

Preheat oven to 350°F. Whisk eggs, yogurt, oil, and vanilla in a large bowl. Add flour, sugar, and baking soda. Stir until smooth. Pour into a greased 9x9 or sheet pan. Bake for 30 minutes or until the center springs back. Cool completely before frosting or serving.

N.V.: Cal. 370 | Fat 16g | Carb. 46g | Prot. 6g

EINKORN CINNAMON SUGAR DONUT HOLES (BAKED)

P.T.: 10 minutes (preparation), 12 minutes (baking)

Ingr.:
- 1 cup all-purpose Einkorn flour
- 1 tsp baking powder
- ¼ tsp salt
- 1 egg
- ⅓ cup milk
- 3 tbsp melted butter
- Cinnamon sugar for rolling

Serv.: 4

Method of Cooking: Oven-baked

Procedure:

Preheat oven to 350°F. Mix flour, baking powder, and salt in a bowl. In another, whisk egg, milk, and butter. Combine wet and dry until smooth. Spoon into mini muffin tins or donut hole pan. Bake 12 minutes. Roll warm bites in cinnamon sugar.

N.V.: Cal. 210 | Fat 9g | Carb. 30g | Prot. 4g

EINKORN S'MORES COOKIE BARS

P.T.: 15 minutes (preparation), 25 minutes (baking)

Ingr.:
- 1¼ cups all-purpose Einkorn flour
- ½ cup coconut sugar
- 1 egg
- ¼ cup butter, softened
- ½ tsp baking soda
- ½ cup dark chocolate chips
- ½ cup mini marshmallows

Serv.: 4

Method of Cooking: Oven-baked

Procedure:

Preheat oven to 350°F. Cream butter, sugar, and egg. Stir in flour and baking soda until dough forms. Fold in chocolate chips and marshmallows. Press into a parchment-lined 8x8 pan. Bake for 25 minutes until golden. Cool slightly before cutting into squares.

N.V.: Cal. 320 | Fat 14g | Carb. 42g | Prot. 5g

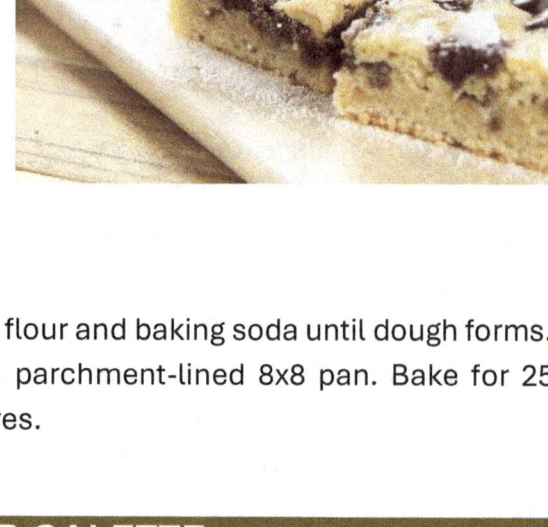

EINKORN PEAR & GINGER GALETTE

P.T.: 25 minutes (preparation), 30 minutes (baking)

Ingr.:
- 1¼ cups all-purpose Einkorn flour
- ½ cup cold butter, cubed
- 3 tbsp ice water
- 2 ripe pears, thinly sliced
- 1 tbsp maple syrup
- ¼ tsp ground ginger
- 1 tsp lemon juice

Serv.: 4

Method of Cooking: Oven-baked

Procedure:

Preheat oven to 375°F. In a bowl, cut butter into flour until crumbly. Add water gradually to form dough. Chill 10 minutes, then roll into a 10-inch circle. Toss pear slices with syrup, ginger, and lemon juice. Layer onto dough, leaving a 1-inch border. Fold edges inward. Bake 30 minutes until golden.

N.V.: Cal. 290 | Fat 15g | Carb. 34g | Prot. 4g

Chapter 7: Nourish & Thrive – Gluten-Sensitive, Allergy-Friendly, and Clean Eating Recipes

EINKORN OAT-FREE ENERGY COOKIES

P.T.: 10 minutes (preparation), 12 minutes (baking)

Ingr.:
- ¾ cup all-purpose Einkorn flour
- ¼ cup sunflower seed butter
- 1 ripe banana
- 2 tbsp chia seeds
- 2 tbsp maple syrup
- 1 tsp vanilla
- ¼ tsp baking soda

Serv.: 4

Method of Cooking: Oven-baked

Procedure:

Preheat oven to 350°F. In a bowl, mash banana and mix with seed butter, syrup, vanilla, and chia seeds. Stir in flour and baking soda until combined. Drop spoonfuls onto a lined sheet and bake 12 minutes until edges are golden.

N.V.: Cal. 200 | Fat 9g | Carb. 28g | Prot. 4g

DAIRY-FREE EINKORN BANANA MUFFINS

P.T.: 10 minutes (preparation), 18 minutes (cooking)

Ingr.:
- 1½ cups all-purpose Einkorn flour
- 1 ripe banana, mashed
- ½ cup unsweetened almond milk
- ½ cup coconut sugar
- 1 tsp baking powder
- 1 egg
- 1 tsp vanilla extract

Serv.: 4

Method of Cooking: Oven-baked

Procedure:

Preheat oven to 350°F. In a bowl, whisk mashed banana, almond milk, egg, and vanilla. Stir in Einkorn flour, coconut sugar, and baking powder until just combined. Divide batter evenly into a lined muffin tin and bake for 18 minutes until a toothpick inserted comes out clean.

N.V.: Cal. 280 | Fat 8g | Carb. 45g | Prot. 7g

EINKORN VEGGIE PATTIES WITH AVOCADO SAUCE

P.T.: 15 minutes (preparation), 12 minutes (cooking)

Ingr.:
- 1 cup grated zucchini (squeezed dry)
- ½ cup grated carrot
- ½ cup all-purpose Einkorn flour
- 1 egg
- 2 tbsp chopped fresh parsley
- 1 ripe avocado
- 1 tbsp lime juice

Serv.: 4

Method of Cooking: Stovetop (pan-fried)

Procedure:

In a bowl, combine zucchini, carrot, Einkorn flour, egg, and parsley. Form mixture into patties. Heat a nonstick skillet over medium heat and lightly spray with oil. Fry patties 6 minutes per side until golden. Meanwhile, mash avocado with lime juice until smooth. Serve patties drizzled with avocado sauce.

N.V.: Cal. 250 | Fat 12g | Carb. 22g | Prot. 8g

LOW-SUGAR EINKORN ZUCCHINI BREAD

P.T.: 12 minutes (preparation), 30 minutes (baking)

Ingr.:
- 1½ cups all-purpose Einkorn flour
- 1 cup grated zucchini (squeezed dry)
- ½ cup unsweetened applesauce
- 1 egg
- 1 tsp baking soda
- 2 tbsp coconut sugar
- 1 tsp cinnamon

Serv.: 4

Method of Cooking: Oven-baked

Procedure:

Preheat oven to 350°F. Whisk egg and applesauce in a bowl, then stir in grated zucchini. In a separate bowl, mix Einkorn flour, baking soda, coconut sugar, and cinnamon. Combine wet and dry ingredients until just mixed. Pour into a greased loaf pan and bake for 30 minutes until a tester comes out clean.

N.V.: Cal. 230 | Fat 5g | Carb. 38g | Prot. 6g

EINKORN BREAKFAST BARS WITH SUNFLOWER SEEDS

P.T.: 10 minutes (preparation), 20 minutes (baking)

Ingr.:
- 1 cup all-purpose Einkorn flour
- ½ cup rolled oats
- ¼ cup sunflower seeds
- ¼ cup mashed banana
- 2 tbsp maple syrup
- 1 egg
- ¼ cup unsweetened almond milk

Serv.: 4

Method of Cooking: Oven-baked

Procedure:

Preheat oven to 350°F. In a bowl, mix mashed banana, egg, almond milk, and maple syrup. Stir in Einkorn flour, oats, and sunflower seeds until a thick batter forms. Spread evenly in a greased 8×8-inch pan and bake for 20 minutes. Cool completely before cutting into bars.

N.V.: Cal. 250 | Fat 8g | Carb. 35g | Prot. 7g

EINKORN "CHEESY" PASTA BAKE (DAIRY-FREE)

P.T.: 15 minutes (preparation), 25 minutes (baking)

Ingr.:
- 2 cups cooked Einkorn penne
- 1 cup tomato sauce
- ½ cup unsweetened cashew cream
- 3 tbsp nutritional yeast
- 1 tsp dried oregano
- 1 garlic clove, minced
- Salt and pepper to taste

Serv.: 4

Method of Cooking: Oven-baked

Procedure:

Preheat oven to 375°F. In a bowl, combine cooked penne, tomato sauce, cashew cream, nutritional yeast, oregano, garlic, salt, and pepper. Transfer to a greased baking dish and bake for 25 minutes until bubbly.

N.V.: Cal. 330 | Fat 10g | Carb. 50g | Prot. 10g

EINKORN LENTIL SLOPPY JOES

P.T.: 12 minutes (preparation), 15 minutes (cooking)

Ingr.:
- 1 cup cooked lentils
- ½ cup tomato sauce
- 1 small onion, finely diced
- 1 tsp Worcestershire sauce (gluten-free if needed)
- 1 tbsp maple syrup
- ½ tsp smoked paprika
- 4 mini Einkorn buns

Serv.: 4

Method of Cooking: Stovetop

Procedure:

In a skillet, sauté diced onion until translucent. Add cooked lentils, tomato sauce, Worcestershire sauce, maple syrup, and smoked paprika. Simmer for 10–15 minutes until thickened. Spoon mixture onto mini buns and serve immediately.

N.V.: Cal. 300 | Fat 3g | Carb. 50g | Prot. 12g

GLUTEN-LIGHT EINKORN WRAPS WITH HUMMUS & VEGGIES

P.T.: 10 minutes (preparation), 5 minutes (cooking)

Ingr.:
- 1½ cups whole grain Einkorn flour
- ½ cup warm water
- 1 tbsp olive oil
- 1 tsp salt
- ½ cup hummus
- 1 cup mixed sliced veggies (bell peppers, cucumbers, carrots)
- 1 tbsp lemon juice

Serv.: 4

Method of Cooking: Skillet

Procedure:

Mix Einkorn flour, water, olive oil, and salt to form a soft dough. Divide into 6 balls and roll out thinly into wraps. Cook each on a hot dry skillet for 1–2 minutes per side until lightly browned. Spread hummus on each wrap, layer with sliced veggies, drizzle with lemon juice, and roll up.

N.V.: Cal. 220 | Fat 8g | Carb. 35g | Prot. 7g

EINKORN & CHICKPEA PROTEIN BITES

P.T.: 10 minutes (preparation), 0 minutes (no-cook)

Ingr.:
- 1 cup canned chickpeas, rinsed and mashed
- ½ cup all-purpose Einkorn flour
- 2 tbsp almond butter
- 2 tbsp coconut sugar
- 1 tsp vanilla extract
- 1 tbsp chia seeds
- 2 tbsp water (adjust for consistency)

Serv.: 4

Method of Cooking: No-cook, chilled

Procedure:

In a bowl, mix mashed chickpeas, almond butter, coconut sugar, vanilla extract, chia seeds, and water until the mixture binds. Refrigerate for 30 minutes, then scoop into small bite-sized balls. Chill further if desired before serving.

N.V.: Cal. 250 | Fat 10g | Carb. 30g | Prot. 8g

EINKORN SPRING ROLL BOWLS WITH GINGER DRESSING

P.T.: 15 minutes (preparation), 0 minutes (cooking)
Ingr.:
- 1 cup cooked Einkorn
- ½ cup shredded red cabbage
- ½ cup julienned carrots
- ½ cucumber, sliced
- 1 tbsp sesame seeds
- 2 tbsp rice vinegar
- 1 tsp fresh grated ginger

Serv.: 4
Method of Cooking: No-cook
Procedure:

In a bowl, layer Einkorn, cabbage, carrots, and cucumber. Whisk rice vinegar and ginger together for a quick dressing. Drizzle over bowls and sprinkle with sesame seeds. Chill or serve immediately.
N.V.: Cal. 210 | Fat 5g | Carb. 34g | Prot. 5g

EINKORN SWEET POTATO BREAKFAST HASH

P.T.: 10 minutes (preparation), 20 minutes (cooking)
Ingr.:
- 1 medium sweet potato, diced
- 1 small zucchini, diced
- ½ cup cooked Einkorn berries
- 1 tbsp olive oil
- ¼ tsp smoked paprika
- Salt and pepper to taste
- Fresh parsley for garnish

Serv.: 4
Method of Cooking: Skillet
Procedure:

Heat olive oil in a skillet over medium heat. Add diced sweet potato and cook 10 minutes, stirring occasionally. Add zucchini, cooked Einkorn, paprika, salt, and pepper. Cook another 8–10 minutes until veggies are tender and slightly crisp. Garnish with fresh parsley.
N.V.: Cal. 230 | Fat 9g | Carb. 34g | Prot. 5g

EINKORN NOODLE STIR-FRY WITH COCONUT AMINOS

P.T.: 12 minutes (preparation), 12 minutes (cooking)

Ingr.:
- 2 cups cooked Einkorn noodles
- 1 cup chopped broccoli
- ½ cup shredded carrots
- 1 tbsp sesame oil
- 2 tbsp coconut aminos
- 1 tsp rice vinegar
- 1 tsp grated fresh ginger

Serv.: 4

Method of Cooking: Stovetop stir-fry

Procedure:

Heat sesame oil in a large skillet or wok. Add broccoli and carrots and sauté for 5 minutes. Add cooked noodles, coconut aminos, rice vinegar, and ginger. Toss well and stir-fry for another 5–7 minutes until everything is warm and coated.

N.V.: Cal. 270 | Fat 9g | Carb. 38g | Prot. 6g

EINKORN FLATBREAD TACOS (ALLERGY-FRIENDLY SHELLS)

P.T.: 15 minutes (preparation), 10 minutes (cooking)

Ingr.:
- 1½ cups whole grain Einkorn flour
- ½ tsp salt
- ½ cup water
- 1 tbsp olive oil
- 1 cup seasoned black beans
- ½ cup mashed avocado
- ½ cup shredded lettuce

Serv.: 4

Method of Cooking: Skillet

Procedure:

Mix Einkorn flour, salt, water, and olive oil into a soft dough. Divide and roll into small flatbreads. Cook on a dry skillet 1–2 minutes per side. Fill each with beans, avocado, and lettuce. Serve warm or room temp.

N.V.: Cal. 260 | Fat 8g | Carb. 36g | Prot. 8g

EINKORN CARROT-APPLE SNACK CAKE (NO REFINED SUGAR)

P.T.: 12 minutes (preparation), 30 minutes (baking)

Ingr.:
- 1 cup grated carrot
- ½ cup grated apple
- 1 cup all-purpose Einkorn flour
- ¼ cup maple syrup
- ¼ cup avocado oil
- 1 egg
- ½ tsp cinnamon

Serv.: 4

Method of Cooking: Oven-baked

Procedure:

Preheat oven to 350°F. In a large bowl, whisk egg, maple syrup, and oil. Stir in carrot, apple, flour, and cinnamon. Pour into a greased 8x8-inch pan and bake for 30 minutes or until center is set. Cool before slicing.

N.V.: Cal. 240 | Fat 10g | Carb. 32g | Prot. 5g

EINKORN CHIA SEED PUDDING CUPS WITH CRUMBLE TOPPING

P.T.: 5 minutes (preparation), 2 hours (chill)

Ingr.:
- 1½ cups unsweetened almond milk
- ¼ cup chia seeds
- 1 tbsp maple syrup
- ½ tsp vanilla extract
- ¼ cup cooked Einkorn flakes
- 1 tbsp sunflower seed butter
- 1 tbsp unsweetened shredded coconut

Serv.: 4

Method of Cooking: No-cook

Procedure:

In a bowl, stir together almond milk, chia seeds, maple syrup, and vanilla. Let rest 5 minutes, then stir again. Cover and refrigerate at least 2 hours or overnight. Before serving, mix Einkorn flakes, seed butter, and coconut to create a crumble topping. Spoon pudding into cups and top with crumble.

N.V.: Cal. 210 | Fat 11g | Carb. 22g | Prot. 6g

EINKORN GREEN VEGGIE FRITTERS

P.T.: 10 minutes (preparation), 10 minutes (cooking)

Ingr.:
- 1 cup grated zucchini
- ½ cup chopped spinach
- ½ cup all-purpose Einkorn flour
- 1 egg
- ½ tsp garlic powder
- Salt to taste
- Olive oil for skillet

Serv.: 4

Method of Cooking: Pan-fried

Procedure:

Squeeze excess moisture from zucchini. In a bowl, combine all ingredients to form a thick batter. Heat oil in a nonstick skillet. Drop spoonfuls into pan and flatten slightly. Cook 3–4 minutes per side until crisp and golden.

N.V.: Cal. 220 | Fat 9g | Carb. 27g | Prot. 6g

EINKORN BLACK BEAN BURGER SLIDERS

P.T.: 15 minutes (preparation), 12 minutes (cooking)

Ingr.:
- 1 cup cooked black beans, mashed
- ½ cup all-purpose Einkorn flour
- 1 tbsp flaxseed meal
- ½ tsp cumin
- Salt and pepper to taste
- 4 mini Einkorn buns
- ½ avocado, sliced

Serv.: 4

Method of Cooking: Pan-seared

Procedure:

In a bowl, mix mashed beans, flour, flaxseed, cumin, salt, and pepper. Form into small patties. Cook on a skillet with a little oil, 5–6 minutes per side. Serve on mini buns with avocado slices.

N.V.: Cal. 290 | Fat 8g | Carb. 39g | Prot. 10g

EINKORN ALMOND-FREE "GRANOLA" CLUSTERS

P.T.: 10 minutes (preparation), 18 minutes (baking)

Ingr.:
- 1 cup puffed Einkorn
- ¼ cup sunflower seeds
- ¼ cup pumpkin seeds
- 2 tbsp maple syrup
- 1 tbsp sunflower seed butter
- 1 tsp cinnamon
- Pinch of salt

Serv.: 4

Method of Cooking: Oven-baked

Procedure:

Preheat oven to 325°F. Mix all ingredients in a bowl until coated. Spread onto a parchment-lined sheet and press gently to form clumps. Bake 18 minutes until crisp. Cool completely before breaking into clusters.

N.V.: Cal. 230 | Fat 10g | Carb. 28g | Prot. 5g

Chapter 8: The Einkorn Lifestyle – Meal Planning, Storage, and Long-Term Success

Einkorn works best when it becomes part of your rhythm, not a special occasion project. The goal isn't perfection—it's consistency, flexibility, and food that feels real. Whether you're planning meals, freezing extras, or baking with your kids, these small choices shape a way of eating that actually fits your life.

How to Plan a Weekly Einkorn Menu for the Whole Family

A weekly menu built around Einkorn isn't about making everything from scratch or baking every day. It's about setting rhythms that work with real life—school mornings, late workdays, unexpected moods, and a fridge that always seems a little emptier than you thought. If you want Einkorn to be more than a once-a-week experiment, it has to be woven into your routine in a way that feels manageable, flexible, and actually enjoyable.

Start by anchoring the week around the meals you already know your family eats. Don't reinvent breakfast, lunch, and dinner all at once. Take your go-to meals—the ones your kids will eat without negotiation—and ask yourself where Einkorn can naturally replace what you're already using. Pancakes? Switch in Einkorn. Sandwiches? Bake a simple sandwich loaf on Sunday. Pasta night? Einkorn flour makes hearty, hand-rolled noodles if you've got the time—or use Einkorn crackers on the side of a soup if you don't.

Think in categories, not individual recipes. Have one or two breakfast options prepped that hold for a few days. Batches of muffins, waffles that reheat well in the toaster, or a breakfast bake that slices like a casserole. For lunch, leftovers and cold meals are your friend. Einkorn wraps, hand pies, or frittata muffins hold up well and pack easily. Dinner is where most families either thrive or give up, so make it realistic. One night of baking—maybe pizza night with Einkorn crust—and a couple meals where Einkorn is just part of the dish, not the focus.

Snack time is often overlooked, but this is where Einkorn shines in a family setting. Baked snack bars, soft cookies, crackers—they're easy to make in bulk, and they give kids a sense of connection to the food they eat. When snacks come from your kitchen instead of a box, kids notice. They may not say anything, but they notice.

Planning a menu doesn't mean committing to it like a contract. Some weeks, everything flows. Other weeks, the plan falls apart on Tuesday. The trick is to have a few fallback options baked and frozen ahead of time—a loaf of bread, a tray of muffins, a couple single-serve breakfast bakes. These give you breathing room when life turns sideways.

Einkorn fits best into a family when you stop trying to make it perfect and start making it consistent. A little here, a little there, and suddenly it's not a project—it's just how you eat. That shift doesn't happen through one spectacular dinner. It happens when Einkorn shows up again and again—on the plate, in the lunchbox, at the table—without needing to be announced. It becomes the grain that lives with you. Not the one that waits for a free weekend.

Einkorn Batch Cooking: What Freezes Well (and What Doesn't)

Batch cooking with Einkorn can save your week—or wreck a good bake—depending on what you freeze and how you do it. Einkorn isn't like standard wheat. It has less gluten, higher natural fats, and a softness that's beautiful fresh but fragile in the freezer. That means you've got to know which recipes hold up and which ones fall apart, dry out, or lose their magic after a few days on ice.

Let's start with the winners. Einkorn waffles and pancakes freeze beautifully. Their dense, tender crumb stays moist, and they reheat with almost no loss of flavor. Wrap them tight, lay them flat, and warm them up in the toaster or oven. Muffins and quick breads also do well—especially those with a bit of fat, fruit, or moisture built in. A banana muffin, an applesauce breakfast cake, or a pumpkin loaf will hold their texture and flavor without drying out. Cookies? Totally freezer-friendly, both baked and unbaked. Pop raw dough balls in a freezer bag and bake straight from frozen. They actually benefit from the cold.

Then you've got bread—and this is where it gets trickier. A fresh Einkorn loaf is heavenly the day it's made, still solid the day after, but by day three it either goes dry or dense, and freezing doesn't always rescue it. If you want to freeze bread, slice it first. Wrap the slices individually or stack them with parchment between each piece. That way you can pull out what you need without thawing the whole loaf. Whole loaves? Risky. You'll almost always lose that delicate interior texture that makes Einkorn so special.

Pizza dough can go either way. If it's got a long, slow rise and enough hydration, you can freeze it in single-use portions with decent results. But anything low-moisture or with a short ferment might come out flat and uncooperative. You'll end up fighting the dough instead of stretching it.

Savory pies and casseroles made with Einkorn crusts or toppings have to be approached with care. Freeze them after assembly, not after baking, and only if the filling isn't too wet. Einkorn crust doesn't hold up well under heavy, watery fillings once thawed—it soaks and slumps instead of staying flaky. And never freeze batters that rely on whipped egg whites, sourdough activity, or steam for lift. They'll collapse before they even get to the oven.

What works with Einkorn in the freezer is all about balance—fat, moisture, structure. If you bake something dry, delicate, or lean, it won't freeze like its modern wheat counterpart. But if you get the texture right, protect it well, and don't overdo the storage time, Einkorn can be just as batch-friendly as any other grain. Maybe even more so, once you understand what it needs—and what it can't fake.

Storing Einkorn Grains and Flour for Maximum Freshness

Einkorn isn't built for sitting around. It's a living, delicate grain with real oils and real flavor—nothing bleached, nothing stripped, nothing buffered by shelf-stable science. That means how you store it matters just as much as how you bake with it. One wrong choice—too much light, too much air, a humid cabinet—and the flour that smelled nutty and warm when you bought it suddenly turns flat, bitter, even rancid. It doesn't take long. And once that freshness is gone, you can't bake your way back to it.

Start with whole Einkorn berries. Unmilled grain is much more forgiving than flour, but it's still vulnerable. The oils are tucked inside, protected by the bran, so you've got a little more wiggle room. But heat, moisture, and bugs don't care. A sealed, food-grade container in a cool, dark pantry works for short-term storage. Long-term? Tuck it in the freezer. Not just for emergencies or bulk buyers—if you live somewhere warm or don't bake every week, the freezer extends shelf life dramatically without changing texture or milling behavior. Just bring it to room temp before grinding, or you'll gum up your mill.

Freshly ground Einkorn flour, or store-bought flour from a trusted source, is where things get more fragile. Once the flour's exposed—bran cracked, oils open—it starts aging. Fast. That beautiful golden hue and soft, clean aroma? They fade within weeks if the flour's left on a warm counter or in a glass jar by the stove. You might not smell the change right away, but you'll taste it. Your muffins will flatten. Your pancakes will have an odd aftertaste. It's subtle, but once you know what to look for, you'll never ignore it again.

Keep your Einkorn flour in airtight containers, away from light, preferably in the fridge or freezer. If you're baking multiple times a week, a cool pantry might be enough. But most home kitchens run warmer than people realize. That cozy, well-lit shelf above the oven? Worst spot in the house. Cold storage isn't just a safety move—it protects the flavor, the texture, the performance. And since Einkorn isn't cheap, every ounce deserves that protection.

If you buy in bulk, divide it. Keep what you'll use in the next couple weeks accessible, and freeze the rest in smaller portions. You don't want to be thawing and re-freezing flour over and over. The more it's exposed to air and moisture, the faster it breaks down. And moisture is sneaky—it can creep in from condensation even inside the fridge. That's why containers matter. No zip-top bags. No open paper sacks. Think tight seals. Think consistency.

Einkorn rewards attention. It doesn't need luxury or special equipment, but it does need care. And once you dial in your storage system, the flour will show up ready—every time—with the smell, the taste, and the strength you expect from a grain that still remembers where it came from.

Building a Family Einkorn Routine with Kids

If you want Einkorn to become part of your family's real life—not just your pantry—you have to build it in. Not just around the recipes, but around the people who live with those recipes. That means involving kids, without overwhelming them. Making space for mistakes. Letting food become something they touch, mix, taste, and talk about, not just something that shows up on a plate without explanation. Einkorn gives you that opportunity. Not every grain does.

Start with presence, not perfection. Kids don't need to become mini bakers. They just need to see it happen. Let them scoop the flour, even if it spills. Let them stir the batter, even if it's lumpy. Give them a corner of dough to fold or shape—imperfect loaves make better memories than flawless ones they weren't allowed to touch. When kids connect with a food in their hands, they're far more likely to try it with their mouths. They begin to recognize it. Not just as something "healthy," but as something familiar. Something theirs.

Routine isn't about locking into rigid schedules. It's about consistency they can count on. Maybe Friday is Einkorn pancake day. Maybe Sunday is baking day. Maybe they help pack Einkorn muffins into school lunches. Whatever the rhythm, it doesn't need to be big. It just needs to repeat. Repetition is how food becomes culture inside a home—not through lectures, but through experience.

Be honest with them about what Einkorn is. Not in a preachy, "this is good for you" way. But in a grounded, curious way. Show them the color difference in the flour. Let them smell it. Talk about how it behaves differently from the flour they've seen before. Kids don't need everything simplified. They just need to be let in. When they're part of the process, they're more invested in the outcome.

You'll hit pushback. Some weeks they won't want the muffins they loved last week. Some days the texture won't be right. Some attempts will flop. That's part of the rhythm too. Teaching your kids that food isn't always flawless is one of the greatest gifts you can offer. Einkorn will help you do that, because it's not built for mass-market perfection. It's meant to be touched, shaped, tasted, and—sometimes—improved over time.

And when it becomes normal, when Einkorn is just what bread looks like in your house or what waffles taste like on Saturday, that's when you know the routine has taken hold. Not because they memorize the recipes, but because they stop questioning why the flour is golden. They just reach for it like it's always been there. That's how a lifestyle forms—quietly, repeatedly, together.

Scan the QR CODE to access the BONUS

www.ingramcontent.com/pod-product-compliance
Lightning Source LLC
Chambersburg PA
CBHW081406070526
44583CB00020B/2699